# THE CHURCH
# AND THE CHURCH SCHOOL

# THE CHURCH and THE CHURCH SCHOOL

A Text-Book Study of the Church Organized
for Religious Education

*KEYSTONE STANDARD TRAINING COURSE*

*By*
WILLIAM EVERETT CHALMERS

———

PHILADELPHIA
THE JUDSON PRESS

| BOSTON | CHICAGO | LOS ANGELES |
| KANSAS CITY | SEATTLE | TORONTO |

Printed in U. S. A.

THIS BOOK IS DEDICATED

TO

MY WIFE AND COWORKER

TO WHOSE INSPIRATION
AND ABUNDANT LABORS
IT OWES ITS EXISTENCE

# FOREWORD

THIS book is one of a series of training text-books designed to equip the student for the teaching ministry of the church. It is to be used in connection with a study of the pupil, a study of teaching principles, a study of the Old and New Testaments, and a study of Christianity as a way of life and belief. This book seeks to give the student a view of the church as an educational agency, and to show how and why the church must organize to teach.

NOTE.—The quotation on page 82, from "Education of the Pueblo Child," by F. C. Spencer, is used by the kind permission of the publishers, the University of Columbia Press.

# CONTENTS

# I

## THE CHURCH MUST TEACH

The small child is an animated question-mark. Insistently it assails mother's ears with "Why?" Sometimes that demand for a reason must be met by an affirmation of sheer authority which does not choose to give the reason why. Immaturity could not understand, and the earliest requirement is for submission to superior authority. But as immaturity develops reasoning powers a wise authority takes time to explain the reasons behind commands, for with an understanding of the reasons binding upon officer and private alike, obedience becomes intelligent and whole-hearted.

As small children we were marshaled by the church into a class under the control of a teacher. We accepted the situation without challenge, for we were at the submissive age. Now we have come to the time of mature questioning, and ask, Why must the church teach? If we can obtain an answer to this question, we believe we can understand better how the church must prepare itself to teach effectively.

### Every Individual Needs Religious Education

No one who has observed children and young people sympathetically can have any question about their need of education. Not only do they need general education, but they and adults need religious education. This double need is evident, since

1

### 1. Growing Minds Ask Questions

Young minds, full of activity, normally ask questions. When contact is made with a big, vital truth or with a commanding personality, minds are stimulated beyond the ordinary. It is impossible to escape the responsibility of carrying forward the education of a mind aroused by the startling entrance of a great truth. The aroused mind insists upon someone taking an interest in its education.

The need of an education is further established by the fact that

### 2. Knowledge Expands Horizons

The Master of Life has come to enable men to live in a large way. He meets the petty, imprisoned soul as an emancipator. New knowledge releases from ignorance, prejudice, fear. Patiently the true teacher brings the light which reveals the world beautiful and solicits the adventurous soul to explore the regions beyond.

Present-day education is emphasizing pupil activity because

### 3. Applied Knowledge Develops Personality

Every baby coming into the world brings the beginnings of a personality. The culture and growth of personality is a first responsibility of the individual. Parents and teachers can only assist. In the measure in which a soul receives truth and puts it into practise, it builds truth into life and makes life strong and beautiful.

Education in its larger aspect must include all life. True education must be religious, not only because man needs religion but preeminently because

### 4. God Ever Seeks to Reveal Himself to Man

If the Prodigal Son had gone into a far country of the International Postal Union his father would have written him a letter, probably many letters. The heavenly Father yearns to make himself and his affection known to his earthly children. Not only does he use nature and the Bible to speak to boys and girls and young people and old people, but he also sends teachers to widen their horizons and help them build his truth into their lives. This is the mighty impulse behind all religious education.

## The State Cannot Teach Religion

As civilization becomes more complex it becomes necessary to give the child an increasing body of specialized knowledge and skill. The home becomes unable to meet this demand. Organized society, through the state, supplements the training by parents through the institution of the school. In a democracy the common school becomes a compulsory public school. Public sentiment now insists that all the children of all the people attend school regularly until they are sixteen years of age, or at least until they are fourteen. Since religion is an essential part of a child's education the simplest plan would be to have the public school teach religion. In order to understand the reason why the American public school cannot teach religion we must review the growth of education in our country.

### 1. The Early Public Schools Were Religious

The early white settlers on the American continent came seeking civil and religious liberty. In many instances re-

ligious persecution or its threat was the immediate cause
of the migration. The colonists, particularly in New England, built the church house and the schoolhouse among
their earliest undertakings. The preacher in the church
on Sunday became the schoolmaster during the week. The
text-books were largely devoted to Bible stories and to the
catechism. In 1642 the Massachusetts General Court
ordered, " That all masters of families do, once a week at
least, catechise their children and servants in the grounds
and principles of religion." Five years later the Bay
Colony ordered townships of fifty householders to establish
public schools which made religious instruction as essential as teaching to read and write.

## 2. American Public Schools Became Secularized

In the European countries from which the settlers came
the established church controlled education. Dissenters
felt the heavy hand of ecclesiastical tyranny when they
sought to save their children from the teaching of religious
doctrines in which they did not believe. These memories
strengthened the purpose of the colonists to keep education free.

Among the first ten amendments to the Constitution,
commonly called the Bill of Rights, was a provision for
the separation of Church and State. The application of
this amendment to public-school control became apparent.
In 1805 New York State forbade the teaching of religion
in the public schools, and provided that children could be
dismissed for one-half day a week for religious instruction upon request by the parents.

As immigration increased and came from many countries with quite different religious backgrounds, it became

necessary to guard the community school from any suggestion of sectarian control. Strong church groups opposed the public school even to the length of building separate parochial schools, but such is the American devotion to a free school that the public school has steadily grown in power and usefulness. This growth was possible only by avoiding religious affiliations or leanings.

Unfortunately the Christian churches of various names have not been able to agree upon the essential elements of all religious training. The public school is without religious material acceptable to all religious people. The school is not irreligious, because our educational leaders generally desire some recognition of religion in the conduct of the school. We expect of the school a respectful attitude toward religious things, but we cannot expect a religious training which Christian parents will deem adequate.

## 3. It Is Evident that the Tax-supported Public School Cannot Teach Religion Adequately

Because of the American principle of the separation of Church and State. That principle has become firmly imbedded in American life. No division of the church seeking control can be permitted to dictate the policy of the public school.

Because of the sectarian divisions among the churches. If an agreement could be had among all interested parents the public school management would find a way to teach the fundamentals of religion without doing violence to American principles. The serious divisions among the religious people of the community have made this impossible.

Because the public school can do nothing more under

present conditions than present religion in courses of History and Literature. If religion is confined to a scholastic study and cannot be taught in such a way as to lead to actual religious experience, it fails to meet the need of human life.

It follows, therefore, that if the State is prevented from teaching religion, the church must meet this tremendous responsibility for the community.

## Human Society Needs the Christian Teaching

Jesus had much to say about a wonderful social order which he called the Kingdom of Heaven. He had much in his teaching for the individual, but he also made prominent social truth.

### 1. The Church Has a Special Message for the Members of the Family

First in importance among all social institutions is the family. It shapes the ideals and habits and character of the growing child more than all other influences entering its life. The church speaking for its Master has much to say about the relation between husband and wife, and child and parent. It commissions its minister to solemnize marriage as an impressive rite with religious sanctions. It is concerned for the maintenance of family life on a high level and for the care and education of the child.

### 2. The Church Is Concerned About the Moral Standards of the Community

A wholesome community life is a blessing to every member of the community, but especially to the boys and girls. The church is aroused when evils enter the community, especially when they become strongly organized. The church is not interested in politics as such, but is interested in political action which will curb evil forces bent on destruction.

The church is bound to be interested in the amusement question. In a day of commercialized amusements purveyors of entertainment may outrage public decency in their pursuit of the dollar. Some prophet must lift his voice in condemnation of the unclean and encourage every worthy effort toward the clean. A public playground movement for the children of a crowded district ought to have church support. The administration of charity by an organization independent of the church is nevertheless a concern of the church. In its many moral phases the church is interested in the community life.

## 3. The Church Must Consider the Human Factor in Industry

The minister of the church is not expected to be a specialized economist. The Sunday-school teacher is not expected to teach thrift so that the savings-bank can increase its business. But the Lord Jesus will not permit his church to forget the laborer in industry, whether he is a wage-earner or a salaried officer. Modern industry tends to turn men into machines, whether at the bottom or the top. The church is interested in the standards and spirit of industry that it be not turned into a dehumanizing process.

## 4. The Church's Vision Includes International Relations

A significant by-product of the modern missionary movement has been the feeling brought into the church

B

for foreign nations and strange peoples. This broad sympathy for many races with strange customs and culture has opposed a narrow national provincialism and race pride. It has made the church interested in the question of peace or war, in preparations for war, and in the settlement of international questions according to the principles of Jesus.

## The Church of Today Must Build the Church of Tomorrow by Teaching

The teaching ministry of the church has no task more important than the training of leaders and workers for the church of tomorrow. This is evident from the emphasis in Jesus' earthly ministry and from the significant place of young people in the church.

### *1. The Twelve Disciples Were Carefully Trained*

Jesus had a very brief public ministry. It covered less than three years. A considerable part of his time and effort was spent with a few men. He chose them carefully and prayerfully. He formed them into a training-class and gave them his first attention, because they were to carry on his work.

### *2. The Young People of Today Are Determining the Church of Tomorrow*

Is the future church to have an intelligent and loyal membership? Ask the young people of today. Is the future church to have a competent and devoted leadership? Ask the young people of today. The attention which is paid to the young people will be more than repaid in the blessings to flow into and from the coming church.

### 3. *The Church Must Summon a Specialized Training Ministry*

The public school has advanced to its present standards because of the efficient and progressive normal school. The church must train its ministers with care. The church must also train its lay leadership. To accomplish this it needs a department of leadership training. The splendid body of volunteer church workers are not only carrying the big load of church work today, but are fixing the character of the future church.

## Christ Commands Teaching

If the church understood no other reason for teaching the imperative of her Lord would be sufficient. He who said, " All authority is given unto me in heaven and on earth," also said, " Go ye therefore, teaching them to observe all things which I commanded you." In order to feel the force of this mighty imperative let us look at his example and at his explicit commands.

### 1. *His Own Example*

The common title to which Jesus responded was " Rabbi "—teacher. (John 1:38, 49; 3:2, 26.) We find him taking the position of an Eastern teacher (Matt. 5:1) before a large company of hearers, before the select group of his disciples (John 9:2; 11:8), and before individuals. (John 3:2; 4:9ff.)

### 2. *His Explicit Command to Preach*

Jesus had good news—a gospel to proclaim. (Luke 4: 18.) So he constituted the Twelve (Luke 9:1) and the

Seventy (Luke 10:9) " messengers." The Great Commission (Mark 16:15) was first of all a command to "herald" the "good news." This command to proclaim publicly he repeats in a variety of forms. (Matt. 24:14.) In the language which Jesus used the preacher must think of himself as a messenger and as a herald.

### 3. His Equally Explicit Command to Teach

Jesus in his own practise combined the method of a public proclaimer carrying on the work of John the Baptist (Mark 1:14), with the method of a teacher before a group ready to be formed into a class of learners. (Matt. 4:23.) While the first method of public announcement is the mere communication of knowledge, the second method signifies that "closer instruction which examines the subject." As he developed his work a band of learners (disciples) was formed whom he separated from those who remained uncommitted to him (Mark 3:13) in order to give them the careful instruction befitting an enlisted learner. Hence his command to those who are to carry on his work is to persuade men to become disciples, enrol them as learners in order that they may receive the careful instruction which his trained disciples must make ready to impart, by the aid of the spirit of truth, their Helper. (Matt. 28:19, 20.)

Since many are influenced by the public preaching in shaping their idea of the teacher it is well to sharpen the distinctions between the two by noting some characteristics of good teaching which are not true necessarily of good preaching. Sunday-school teachers often attempt to be little preachers. It will help us if we pause to note some differences.

### 4. In Christ's Double Command We Must Distinguish Between Teaching and Preaching

(1) Good Teaching Must Be Consecutive. Each lesson is built upon the preceding and prepares for the following. There is a general lesson theme or subject which is analyzed and organized comprehensively. Teaching insists upon regular attendance and continuous application to a single line of thought. Preaching may be effective in presenting themes which have no connection or only a very general connection. The morning subject may give no indication of the evening subject. The sermon subject one week may have nothing to do with the subjects for the following week. Indeed, many homiletical authorities maintain that variety of subject strengthens preaching.

(2) Good Teaching Expects Previous Study. On the first day of the new term the class meets the teacher without a prepared lesson. At that first class session the teacher assigns a portion of the work which must be completed before the class meets again. Good teaching is more the directing of pupil study than the delivery of learned disquisitions. The lack of class study makes good teaching impossible. The preacher can expect no such preparation on the part of the congregation. If they are willing to come and listen attentively with an open mind, he counts himself fortunate. Preaching has the more difficult task of interesting unprepared minds and drawing them together about a common subject of thought.

(3) Good Teaching Grades Pupils. No teacher can be quite happy in an ungraded school. He discovers speedily that differing degrees of maturity and immaturity, differing abilities and differing developments, demand separate

treatment and unlike material. The true teacher must insist on dividing pupils into separate groups, even if they must be small groups, so that each group stands upon an approximately common intellectual level. The preacher must face an ungraded company. The church door swings easily before any comer without respect to age or intellectual or spiritual attainment. It is no easy task to find subjects which will interest every one who attends and develop them in such a way as to hold attention and give a general helpfulness. Grading is a help which must be given to the teacher but cannot be extended to the preacher. Good teaching demands careful grading.

(4) Good Teaching Invites Pupil Participation. It is possible for a teacher to talk too much. It is possible for a teacher to leave pupils undeveloped because he insists on making the entire lesson presentation. Such a teacher states all the problems and announces all the solutions. Such a classroom method fails to understand that teaching is a social affair—a partnership affair in which the gains accrue to those who take part. Preaching depends for its effectiveness in no small part upon its association with a formal service of worship. Any interruption of a solemn worship program would be resented as a rudeness and impiety by the assembled worshipers. This quiescent, submissive attitude carries over into the sermon period. It would wake up some sleepy congregations, and possibly stir up some preachers if the old synagogue custom prevailed of asking the preacher questions.

(5) Good Teaching Secures Class and School Organization. A teacher is concerned to help his pupils to a regular attendance and to a group loyalty. He makes a class-roll, establishes a definite class-membership, asks at each

session who are absent and why. As pupils grow in a sense of responsibility, he tactfully encourages the selection of leaders who are charged with the interests of the class as a social unit. Naturally the growing social feeling reaches beyond the class to other classes, the sharing of a common organization, the building of the department and school.

## 5. *Christ's Command to Teach Is Always Associated with His Command to Evangelize*

In the practise of Jesus teaching always accompanied evangelism. When he met the Samaritan woman at the wellside he first proceeded to instruct her in preparation for the disclosure of himself as the Messiah, in order to bring about a complete readjustment of her life to righteousness and to God the Spirit. Before issuing the call " Follow me " to his disciples he makes sure they have been taught concerning himself, either by his own lips or by John the Baptist. Obedience to his call affects their whole life in all its habits and adjustments.

Sometimes religious education has been understood as a substitute for evangelism. It has been denounced by some evangelists as the introduction of a man-made device in place of the divine work of regeneration. When religious education is true to itself it becomes the ally and helper of true evangelism. It is opposed to a sham evangelism which is satisfied with a superficial and passing emotional experience without a content of enduring truth. It is bound up with a genuine evangelism which introduces to the life glorious and eternal. It maintains that the highest and best evangelism does not wait until the mature man becomes habituated and fixed in ways of sin, but begins with the child and expects to lead the boy and girl to Christ.

## 6. Christ's Command Makes Teaching a Church Responsibility

It is not enough that individuals and groups within the church are trying to teach the ignorant in response to the call of need and the command of Christ. In the next lesson we shall see how the impulse to teach organized certain movements for neglected classes by a portion of the church-membership. Such were the beginnings of the Sunday-school movement, of the woman's movement, of the young people's movement, and others. Nobly have organizations of church people carried on in behalf of special classes. These organizations have grown great and become national and international in their reach. They have fostered organizations within the local church of like name with the parent body. Unintentionally they have promoted disunity within the church and have made it difficult for the church as a church to face its full responsibility.

In this study we propose to ask why the church must have its own leadership in religious education and construct a unified program. We must consider how it can relate its subordinate organizations to each other and to the new leadership which it must establish. We must find a way, if possible, whereby the work of the specialist can be strengthened as he supplies material and expert advice, and at the same time secure a competent church leadership who will make use of all available helps while insisting on the unity of the church task.

If the Church must teach because every individual needs

religious education, because the State cannot teach religion, because society needs the Christian teaching, because the Church of today is building the Church of tomorrow by teaching, and supremely because Christ commands teaching, then the Church must organize itself to teach all classes of folks all they need to learn for a great religious experience.

Durant Drake, in his discussion of " Shall We Stand by the Church?" says:

The church should be a great educational institution giving the great mass of common people insight into the meaning and mystery of life, a clear apprehension of their real needs and duties. It should patiently train its members in the performance of these duties. It should be a center for friendship and human sympathy, a means of ministry to the community, a standing rebuke to the sins of the world, and a lever for attack upon all forms of sin and wrong.[1]

## Help for the Teacher

There are many who have not thought of the church as a teaching agency, so it is necessary to show from the very nature of the child and his needs that he must be taught. Yet in a democracy the State cannot teach religion, but human society needs the Christian teaching, and only by teaching can the Church perpetuate itself. Moreover, a little study will convince one that Jesus commands teaching as well as preaching, and is himself the great Teacher. There is a distinction between preaching and teaching, and the church cannot escape its responsibility for both. It is the church at its educational task that this book is to consider.

[1] Used by permission of the Macmillan Company, owners of the copyright.

### Suggestions for Further Study

1. Discuss the use of the Bible in the public school, its advantages, disadvantages.

2. Make a study of Jesus as a teacher.

3. Make your own list of things to be gained through preaching rather than teaching and vice-versa.

4. Read the Constitution of the United States.

## II

# THE CHURCH HAS BEEN TEACHING

## AN HISTORICAL REVIEW

### Parents the First Teachers

The first and most important religious educators are the parents. In all times and among all people the little child looks up first into mother's face and reads there love and trust in God or fear and hate of the Unseen and Unknown. It is recorded of Abraham (Gen. 18:19), " For I know him, that he will command his children and his household after him." Moses repeatedly enjoined upon the people the duty of the parents to teach the children. (Deut. 6: 7.) No school or church can ever relieve parents of this primal obligation to lead the little child in its first important steps toward a knowledge of God. But it was true of the Hebrews as of other peoples that as a national sense gradually developed among them, the need for more formal instruction was felt. At court there were private teachers. (2 Kings 10:5.) The priests were engaged in teaching. (Micah 3:11.) Ezra read the law while the Levites taught the people. (Neh. 8:9.) These two quotations from the Talmud serve to show the value placed upon teaching among the Hebrews:

" He who has learned and does not impart his knowledge unto others disregards the Word of God."

" He who studies and teaches others possesses treasures and riches."

17

## Historically, After the Parents the Church Becomes the Great Teacher of Religion

When Jesus was a child, every Jewish boy was required to attend the synagogue school. There seated upon the floor they swayed back and forth reciting in repetitious singsong the rich treasures of Hebrew literature. Mere memorizing to some, but to Mary's Son the words opened great avenues of wisdom and beauty and prompted the eager questioning of the learned doctors in his Father's house.

In the very earliest centuries of the Christian era we find the beginnings of the so-called catechetical schools. Unlike the synagogue schools, these were not intended for little children but only for applicants for church-membership. In them the candidate heard read the letters of the apostles and the sayings of Jesus and committed to memory the prayers and hymns of the church. In time these schools came to have quite a definite course covering two years, in which time the candidate advanced from one degree to another. Some very remarkable teachers appeared during these first four centuries, and teaching received more attention than in the succeeding years up to the Renaissance and the Reformation.

Gradually the education offered by the church became more and more formal and was more and more reserved for those studying for the priesthood. Followed those long centuries of midnight ignorance when few even of the priests could read or write, and none had the Bible in his own tongue. When in 1517 Luther nailed his theses to the door of the little Wittenberg church, his hammer struck a blow at special privilege in education and pounded open a door for the coming of the common school. His ambition was to give the Bible to his people in the German vernacular, but his efforts would have been in vain were it not for that other great event, the invention of the printing-press in 1450. Fostered by the church, both Protestant and Roman Catholic schools were founded, from which have grown the modern colleges and universities on the continent and in the British Isles.

By the beginning of the eighteenth century the Bible, once chained to the pulpit, had become free to all. It was possible for all who could afford to pay for it to get an education, and since the schools were so closely allied with the church, one's education included some form of religious instruction. The Massachusetts School Ordinance of 1647 begins, " It being one of the chief projects of that old Deluder, Satan, to keep men from the knowledge of the Scripture," and continues, " that learning may not be buried in the grave of our fathers in the church and the commonwealth," and concludes with provision for the teaching of all the children within given boundaries to read and write. Their text-book was the New England Primer containing Catechism Questions and Answers, the Lord's Prayer, Apostles' Creed, prayers and hymns for children. From these two examples we see that both the impulse for education and the materials of education of colonial days were religious.

## The Influence of Democracy

New theories of education and the growth of the democratic idea were combining to change men's thought as to who should be educated and how. The Declaration of Independence proved to be the greatest brief for universal education ever penned. " There was no way to obtain the education of rich and poor alike save by the government owned school. It is impossible for us to conceive the boldness of the measure which aimed at universal education through the establishment of free schools," said Horace Mann, who was himself one of the great factors in making these schools possible. In a young country fighting with all the force of inward conviction to avoid the evils of a political State under the dominance of a political Church, it was inevitable that the determination should be strong that State schools must be free from Church control. But, even so, had it been possible for our forefathers so far to forget sectarian differences as to agree upon some common basic religious truths to be taught to all the children of all the people, we might not today have the spectacle of a great nation founded by religious people upon the religious impulse rearing her children in entire ignorance of religion.

## Sunday-school Beginnings in the United States

Just about the time it began to be borne in upon thinking people that the religious education of American children was being neglected, word was received in this country of the Ragged Schools founded in Gloucester, England, by Robert Raikes. There were no schools for the common people in England and out of a great pity for the destitute, ignorant children in the streets of his city, Raikes began these Sunday afternoon schools in which the Bible was used to teach the rudiments of reading, writing, and arithmetic. Seizing upon the missionary idea but adapting it to our own need, which was for religious instruction to supplement the work of the public schools, Sunday schools were started in several places. There is some dispute as to where the very first Sunday school was organized in this country. Plymouth and Roxbury, Massachuetts; Ephrata, Pennsylvania; Accomac and Hanover Counties, Virginia, are among those laying claim to the honor. In 1790 the First Day or Sunday School Society was organized in Philadelphia and was interdenominational, the call for its organization having come from an Episcopalian, a Universalist, and a Catholic. In this same year the Methodist Conference of Charleston, South Carolina, gave official recognition to the Sunday schools. In the next few years the movement spread among Protestant churches of all denominations and many local unions of neighboring Sunday-school workers were formed. These schools differed from the Sunday school of Great Britain in three important particulars:

1. They were with a few exceptions approved by the church.

2. They were primarily for religious instruction of the children of the church, rich and poor alike.

3. The teachers were volunteers, unpaid laymen and women.

Gradually these local unions united until in 1824 The American Sunday School Union was organized. It had three objects: (1) Selection and preparation of Sunday-school material, (2) publication of suitable Sunday-school literature, (3) and the missionary work of planting new schools in needy places.

## Subsequent Sunday-school History

For convenience, the succeeding history of the Sunday-school movement may be divided into four periods:

*I. 1824–1860*

1. This period was marked by the spread of the Sunday-school idea and formation of many schools.

2. It was further marked by the growth of State Associations. These were interdenominational in character and fostered by laymen.

3. During these years the various denominations were slowly awakening to the importance of the movement, and denominational Sunday School Boards under various titles were created.

4. Called in the first place by The American Sunday School Union, the beginnings of a National Convention were made. The attendance at first was small, but interest was growing.

*II. 1868–1907*

Interrupted by the Civil War, Sunday-school leaders went at the task with renewed vigor at its close. The next forty years were marked by great progress in the Sunday-school world.

1. At the Convention in Indianapolis, 1872, a system of uniform lessons was adopted and a Lesson Committee appointed. The most enthusiastic promoters of this plan were B. F. Jacobs, Henry Clay Trumbull, and John H. Vincent, three giants in the Sunday-school world.

2. In 1875 the convention met at Baltimore and by the admission of Canada was expanded to become the International Sunday School Association, which became incorporated in 1907.

3. A great step forward was made when the International Sunday School Association reached the place where

it was able to employ a General Secretary. The men who served in that capacity became known and loved throughout the Sunday School World. William Reynolds was made Field Superintendent in 1887, but in 1899 Marion Lawrance became General Secretary and served many years, part of the time as secretary for the World's Sunday School Association also. Under his strong and winsome leadership State and Provincial Associations were developed and a great impetus was given to the Sunday-school cause.

4. In 1889 the first World's Sunday School Convention was called in London, England. Since then conventions have been held in St. Louis, London, Jerusalem, Rome, Washington, Zurich, Tokyo, Glasgow, and in 1928 in Los Angeles. The World's Association is performing a great service in aiding the Sunday-school cause in every land, maintaining trained secretaries on missionary fields, and serving as a medium of exchange of Sunday-school ideals and enthusiasm.

5. As the period to 1824 was one of simple beginnings, this second was one of expansion and increasing perfection of organization. This period also was marked by much discussion and many experiments both as to the material to be used and methods of teaching and organization in the Sunday school.

### III. *1908–1921*

Principally because of the developing ideas in the field of education, this period of Sunday-school history was marked by many changes, not only in lesson material, but in the form of organization of the various associations carrying on Sunday-school work.

c

1. *1894.* It was back in 1894 that a group of teachers of little children formed the International Primary Union and began agitation for lessons suitable for children under six years of age.

2. *1908.* This and other influences led the International Association to instruct its Lesson Committee in 1908 to prepare a graded course, which should be optional with the uniform lessons.

3. *1910.* Denominational Sunday School Boards had been growing stronger and more and more concerned for the extension and welfare of their Sunday schools and the problems involved in administering them. In 1910 these boards, numbering about thirty, formed the Sunday School Council of Evangelical Denominations.

4. *1922.* For several years the leadership of the Sunday schools of North America was divided between two general organizations, the International Sunday School Association and the Sunday School Council of Evangelical Denominations. A merger was finally effected in 1922, and the International Council of Religious Education came into being.

5. The change in the method of teaching led directly to changes in the organization of the Sunday school. This period is marked by the growth of the graded school idea and the great increase in the number of Teacher Training Classes and Institutes.

6. Another marked phase of the latter part of this period has been the growth of the Organized Class, beginning with the adult organizations. In 1890 the first Baraca Class was organized in Syracuse. In March, 1913, the International Sunday School Association reported 35,815 adult classes enrolled.

*IV. 1922 to the Present*

1. Sunday-school architecture is receiving more attention than ever before, and a new type of building adapted to graded work is appearing.

2. Beginning with Robert G. Boville in 1901, the Daily Vacation Bible School idea has grown until it is recognized as an important means of religious education.

3. It was about the year 1910 that several experiments were made in week-day religious instruction, the most notable of these being the Gary Plan, begun in 1913. To-day in the growth of the Week-day Church School we seem to be on the verge of a great forward movement in this type of religious education.

4. The special mark of this present period in Sunday-school history would seem to be, however, the growth of the church-school idea. Raikes' Ragged Schools were opposed by the church as tending to make the poor dissatisfied with their lot. The Sunday school in America had the sympathy and cooperation of the church from the start, but it was a separate institution, often seeming to rival the church in its claim to loyalty. As late as 1913 an outstanding Sunday-school leader, Dr. C. R. Blackall, could write:

> It remains a hard fact that the Sunday school is really an institution outside the church, self-appointed as nursery, " feeder," and " agency," and occupying precisely the same relation to the church as that of the . . . Y. P. S. C. E. and other organizations of similar character, its impetus at all times being exercised from without rather than from within the church.—*Blackall, " Sunday School Situation."*

Only of very late years has the Sunday school been thought of as the church itself at the educational task. The implications of this idea are already at work modifying school management, organization, and teaching methods, so that it seems fair to designate this as the outstanding fact in present-day Sunday-school history.

## Other Educational Agencies of the Church

Great as was the Sunday-school movement, it by no means embraced all of the educational efforts which have engaged the church. A few of these we must now consider.

### 1. *Missionary*

Although, as has been said, the Sunday-school movement was itself in part an outgrowth of the wave of missionary enthusiasm which followed the preaching of Carey in England in 1790 and Adoniram Judson and his colleagues in the United States in 1810, yet the church as a whole has been very slow in realizing the essential missionary character of the gospel. Occasional missionary sermons were preached, but no material was provided for regular missionary instruction. At Kettering, England, the Particular Baptist Society for Propagating the Gospel among the Heathen was organized in 1793. In 1800 the Boston Female Society for Missionary Purposes was organized. Ten years later the American Board of Commissioners for Foreign Missions came into being, and in the years immediately following various denominational missionary boards and societies were organized. Mrs. Caroline Doremus was so impressed by the story of a returned missionary from Assam that she formed in 1861 the Women's Union Missionary Society. Denominational women's foreign missionary societies came soon after. Between the years 1876 and 1893, seventeen women's home mission societies were started. Women's missionary societies were organized in the local churches, and a literature was developed designed to inform the members of the need for missionary work and to appeal for support for the missionary cause. Early in their work the women realized that if the church was ever to become truly missionary, education must begin with the children. Children's societies, junior bands, and young women's guilds were started, and a literature suitable to each was developed. The Student Volunteer Movement was organizd in 1866, and shortly thereafter the first series of missionary text-books was published. There is today a wealth of missionary literature, including study and story-books, hero tales, adventure- and travel-books, maps, leaflets, dramatic presentations, and hymns.

Many schools make a place for the missionary talk or story in the worship period; some teachers make use of missionary illustrative material in their presentation of the lesson; the missionary society gives some training to a limited group. Neither the Sunday-school worker nor the missionary leader is satisfied, however, that a real piece of educational work is being done. Very great improvement may be expected along this line from the findings of committees now at work, under the auspices of the Missionary Education Movement, upon missionary education for different age groups. Some effort has been made to bring into correlation the missionary organizations of the church and the organized classes or departments of the Sunday school, but much more must be done if we are to give to all the church group, young and old, men and women, a full and rounded religious training.

## 2. *Temperance Societies*

Another neglected truth of the church and of Sunday-school teaching was the claim upon the Christian to prac-tise sobriety. As early as 1833 there was held the first National Temperance Convention, but not until the or-ganization of the W. C. T. U. in 1874, following a dis-cussion at a Sunday-school convention, did active propa-ganda for total abstinence begin in the churches. Women's circles, little children's bands, and boys' and girls' clubs were formed. A literature on the subject began to appear, and the Sunday-school lesson committee was finally per-suaded to offer an optional temperance lesson once a quarter.

## 3. *Lend-a-Hand Clubs and Brotherhoods*

As early as 1871 a club of boys was formed, taking for its motto the four precepts of the hero of E. E. Hale's story, " Ten Times One Is Ten ":

> Look up, not down;
> Look forward, not backward;
> Look out and not in;
> Lend a hand.

The idea of personal service in devotion to the Christ ap-pealed strongly, and the movement spread among all de-nominations and all over the world. The International Order of the Kings' Daughters and Sons is an interdenom-inational society started in 1886. It adopted the motto of the Lend-a-Hand Clubs, sounded a strong evangelical note, and grew in 1912 to a membership of 500,000.

The Brotherhood of St. Andrew in the Episcopal Church was followed in 1888 by the Brotherhood of Andrew and

Philip, an interdenominational society placing emphasis upon personal work. The local chapters are expected to help the pastor in all ways to bring men and boys to church.

### 4. Young People's Societies

In the church service the young people were for the most part passive onlookers and listeners. In the Sunday-school class, there was opportunity for something more of give and take, but the initiative was still with the adult. In 1881 Rev. F. E. Clark formed in his own church a Young People's Society of Christian Endeavor modeled upon a Brooklyn society which had impressed him. The characteristic features were a prayer-meeting pledge, the consecration meeting, and the committee work. Societies sprang up in all the churches and great conventions were held.

The United Society has always emphasized loyalty to the local church, but being non-denominational in its control and policies, it was inevitable that denominational organizations along the same lines should arise. The Epworth League of Methodist Young People was formed in 1889, the Baptist Young People's Union of America in 1891, and the Luther League in 1895. Other denominations have organized their young people's societies with separate names or in affiliation with the interdenominational movement.

In some denominational groups an effort has been made to correlate the various young people's organizations which have sprung up in the local church. The Presbyterians have brought together their religious educational and missionary educational leaders in the writing of a unified young people's program. The Baptists also have produced a Christian Life Program for all Baptist young people, in whose promotion the religious education workers, the missionary education workers, and the Baptist Young People's Union of America have united. In several other denominations closer working relationships are being established between young people's groups.

### 5. *Y. M. C. A. and Y. W. C. A.*

The Christian Endeavor Society and the denominational societies along similar lines enlist the young people within the church and have at their heart and center the culture and expression of Christian experience. The Y. M. C. A. and Y. W. C. A. also draw their membership from Christian young people, but have never been church organizations. They seek to promote the mental, moral, social, and physical well-being of young men and young women. The first Y. M. C. A. in this country was organized in Boston in 1851. The Y. W. C. A. was begun in New York in 1858.

### 6. *Boy Scouts, Girl Scouts, Camp Fire Girls*

Influenced by the work of Sir Baden-Powell in England, and of Daniel Carter Beard and Ernest Thompson Seton in this country, the Boy Scouts of America was incorporated in 1910. This is a non-military, non-sectarian organization of boys from 12 to 18 years of age. The boys are organized in patrols of eight, three or four patrols constituting a troop. Each troop has a local council of three men from the school, church, or other institution with which it is connected.

Every Scout must subscribe to the oath:

On my honor I will do my best

(1) To do my duty to God and my country,

(2) To help other people at all times,

(3) To keep myself physically strong, mentally awake, and morally straight.

A Scout is trustworthy, loyal, helpful, friendly, courteous, kind, obedient, cheerful, thrifty, brave, clean, and reverent.

The Girl Scouts are organized along very similar lines. The organization promoted by Dr. Luther H. Gulick and known as the Camp Fire Girls emphasizes more particularly the housewifely virtues. The church furnishes leadership for these groups. All three of these organizations are to be found meeting under church auspices. Their simple ritual together with the concrete demand of specified things to be done makes a strong appeal to boys and girls of the early teens.

To recapitulate very briefly:

As Christian men and women have been impressed with some great neglected truth or neglected group within the church there have come into being organizations designed to meet the need, until today there are missionary societies for women, young women, boys, and girls, and little children, temperance societies, social and recreational clubs, young people's societies, senior, intermediate, and junior, and the organized classes from adult down through young people, intermediate, and junior. These all are doing in a broad sense some phase of religious educational work, in addition to the work of the Sunday school. Each organization has planned its program and carried forward its activities unrelated to other organizations and independent of the church. This has resulted in overlapping and made necessary some plan of correlation.

### Help for the Teacher

This chapter in a brief review of religious educational
agencies in the Christian church seeks to show (1) that
after the primal responsibility of parents the church has
always felt the obligation to teach religion, (2) the reasons
for the rise of the Sunday school in this country, (3) the
spread of the Sunday-school movement with changes in
teaching methods and organization, (4) the history of the
interdenominational Sunday-school movement, (5) neglected truths and areas of service give rise to other organizations doing religious educational work in the church,
(6) the present confused situation.

### Questions for Further Study

1. What organizations are doing educational work in my
local church?

2. Consider one age group in a local church. What
should be included in their religious education?

3. There are in the United States over 1,000 communities supporting Week-day Schools of Religious Education. What is the situation in my own community?

4. Is the one-half hour a week of Sunday-school instruction enough to teach religion adequately?

5. What is the value of a Daily Vacation Bible School?

# OUR AIM IN RELIGIOUS EDUCATION

Having reviewed the obligation which rests upon the church to teach, and having surveyed the attempts of individuals and groups within the church to meet this obligation, we must now make the distinction between individual members and the whole church. The obligation to teach has been placed upon the church as a body, and not alone upon marked individuals. To certain noble souls has come the divine impulse to teach. They have attempted the task separately, or they have associated others with them. Hence has come the splendid Sunday school, young people's, women's, missionary, and other movements within the church.

"I am ready to go into India if you at home will hold the ropes," said Carey. He had discovered that obedience to the divine call to make disciples of every nation involved something additional to individual obedience. The church itself must be organized for the great missionary undertaking.

## Need of an Aim

All attempts to carry forward any part of the task of religious education discover limitations and inefficiencies and competitions until the organized church assumes its proper place of leadership. We have reached the period in the growth of church work when the need of a larger organization and supervision of teaching is facing the

33

church. When the church becomes aroused to undertake a comprehensive plan of religious education, one of the first questions of the new leadership must be: "What is religious education? What are we trying to do? What results are we seeking? What is the aim of religious education?"

When we pause to define our aim, we are seeking simply to act intelligently. Professor John Dewey says:

A man is imperfectly intelligent when he contents himself with looser guesses about the outcome than is needful, just taking a chance with his luck, or when he forms plans apart from study of actual conditions, including his own capacities. . . To have an aim is to act with meaning, not like an automatic machine; it is to *mean* to do something and to perceive the meaning of things in the light of that intent.[1]

Doctor Welton, in his book "What Do We Mean by Education?" says:

The ultimate question is never how to train, but for what to train. Unless the former be consciously related to the latter, the practical work of education can only be ineffective and the theory which underlies that work incoherent and self-destructive.[2]

Dr. Seldon L. Roberts, in his text-book on "Teaching in the Church School," has pointed out the necessity for a teacher's aim:

If the people whom we teach in our church schools are to be Christian in character and conduct there are certain things they must know, there are habits of action which they must form and fix, there are attitudes which they must acquire, there are dispositions of good-will and helpfulness which they must have, relationships which must be understood and willingly assumed, and

[1] "Democracy and Education," 1917; used by permission of the Macmillan Company, owners of the copyright.

[2] Used by permission of the Macmillan Company, owners of the copyright.

there are great loyalties to be developed and sustained. It is the aim of Christian teachers to help people acquire this knowledge, form these habits, and assume by the help of God's grace proper attitudes, relations, and loyalties.[8]

There must also be a church aim big enough for a comprehensive educational scheme. The church must decide upon forms of organization, courses of study, the training of leadership, housing and physical equipment. These decisions will be intelligent in proportion to the clearness with which the church leaders see their objectives. As a help toward the vision of a goal in religious education it would be well to study the nature of education as defined by educational leaders and especially those aims which are influential in contemporary education. This study can be made best as a brief historical review.

## Historical Survery of Educational Aims

The Greeks were the first to appreciate the central importance of personality. Socrates, Plato, and Aristotle sought to harmonize the conflict between the older education whose purpose was the building of a strong state and the new emphasis upon the individual.

The Roman contribution to education was the building of institutions for realizing ideals or social purposes. The Roman mind was practical. At the opening of the Christian era, Greek culture strongly influenced higher education. With the decadence of Rome, the education furnished by the early Christian church gradually replaced the old.

The Middle Ages sought to build a scheme of education upon the Christian religion. Education became dominantly

moral rather than intellectual, hence a discipline or pre-
paratory training.   Monasticism organized moral education with painful minuteness.   The application of logic and
philosophy to theological questions developed scholasticism.
Feudalism produced a special type of education designed
to perpetuate that form of society by training page and
squire in preparation for full knighthood.

The Renaissance was a revolutionary attempt to rescue
the individual.   It was a revolt against the iron rule of
authority in Church, State, industry, society, and education.   Two results followed—a revival of the liberal education of the Greeks, and a narrow humanistic form of
education.   The influence of the Renaissance on education
continued to the beginnings of our own day in the importance given to the classical languages and literatures.   A
purely formal education became identified with liberal education.

The Reformation was both moral and intellectual.   The
earlier effect of the Reformation was to emphasize reason,
the right of private judgment, and acquaintance with
literary sources.   In Protestant countries schools were
taken gradually from the Church and brought under the
control of the State.   The idea of universal education was
born out of the necessity of the individual use of the
Scriptures.   The chief educational significance of the
Reformation is the demand for a universal elementary
education.

This brief review of a development reaching through the
long centuries brings us to the threshold of our own times
and a consideration of the chief theories of education current today and influential in that composite of the years,
modern education.

## Influences in Contemporary Education

### 1. *Contemporary Education Is Influenced by the Disciplinary Theory*

This theory as formulated by the philosopher John Locke made the chief aim of education the development of certain mental abilities, especially memory and reason. It held of little value the information derived from the study of special subjects in comparison with the training which it gave the powers of the mind. Although the theory was based on a faulty psychology of the mind divided into separate " faculties," it contains an element of truth and continues to influence many high schools and colleges.

### 2. *Contemporary Education Is Influenced by the Theory of Naturalism*

The movement for social reform in the eighteenth century, protesting against arbitrary authority in government and religion and the stern schoolmaster who enforced rigidly the disciplinary theory, became known as the Naturalistic Movement. This theory would remove all suppression, reduce instruction to comparatively small consequence, and make the chief aim of education the release or development of natural tendencies. Rousseau gave this theory effective form for education and contributed to modern education the doctrine of interest.

### 3. *Contemporary Education Is Influenced by the Theory of a Harmonious Development of Personality Through Activity.*

Pestalozzi opened new possibilities to popular education by his theory of a balanced development of the child,

physically, intellectually, and morally.  Herbart emphasized the moral aim in education and sought control of
conduct through ideas, thus exalting the teacher and instruction.  Froebel insisted upon the primary importance
of the child, upon self-activity as determining all instruction, and upon play, constructive work, and the study of
nature as the chief means of instruction.

### 4. Contemporary Education Is Influenced by the Theory of Preparation for Complete Living

Herbert Spencer defined the purpose of education as
preparation for complete living.  It must include the ac-
quisition of the most serviceable knowledge and the development of the power to use this knowledge.  Huxley
gave a notable description of a liberal education:

That man has had a liberal education who has been so trained
in youth that his body is the ready servant of his will, and does
with ease and pleasure all the work that as a mechanism it is
capable of; whose intellect is a clear, cold logic engine, with all
its parts of equal strength, and in smooth working order; ready
like a steam-engine to be turned to any kind of work, and spin the
gossamers as well as forge the anchors of the mind; whose mind
is stored with the knowledge of the great and fundamental truths
of nature and of the laws of her operations; one who, no stunted
ascetic, is full of life and fire, but whose passions are trained
to come to heel by a vigorous will, the servant of a tender conscience; who has learned to love all beauty whether of nature
or of art, to hate all vileness, and to respect others as himself.
Such an one and no other has had a liberal education; for he is
as completely as a man can be, in harmony with nature.

The rapid development of the natural sciences during the
nineteenth century introduced as an important preparation
for complete living scientific studies into the curriculum,

at the expense of the old cultural studies. The influence of scientific study is a dominant factor in the education of today.

### 5. *Contemporary Education Is Influenced by the Theory that Education Builds Society*

Democratic statesmen saw that the continuance and growth of the republic depended upon the intelligence of the masses and their instruction in the principles of free government. Education has been conceived as a form of social control. This theory makes education a social process by which one generation transmits the results of its experience to the next. A new social conscience has founded private schools with doors open to all, and driven the state to organize free public schools. This social principle has also led to vocational and industrial training.

## Aims Which Have Influenced the Church in Religious Education

Since the Reformation, and especially since Robert Raikes gathered the street children of Gloucester into the " Ragged School," the church has had a succession of aims for its teachers. We will consider those which have exerted a significant influence.

### *1. To Win Converts*

The churches of the Reformation established themselves on an evangelical basis. Revivals of religion, as in the case of Baptists and Methodists, were principally the winning of converts to Christ as Saviour. We have seen that the command to evangelize has first place in the marching orders of the church, and that religious education must

D

always recognize the chief place of evangelism. In the program of the church school evangelism must have primary consideration. But the winning of converts does not complete the task of religious education. The church has yet many things to do for the child who reaches out to his Saviour in an act of personal faith. It is a serious matter when the church-school leadership lacks the spirit of evangelism. It is also a serious matter when the church has no plan of education beyond evangelism.

## 2. *To Prepare for Death*

The New England Primer was an early text-book of the schools fostered by the church. Dr. A. A. Brown has found this quotation:

> I in the burying place may see
>   Graves shorter there than I.
> From death's arrest no age is free;
>   Young children too may die.
> My God, may such an awful sight
>   Awakening be to me!
> Oh! that by early grace I might
>   For death preparèd be.

The serious Puritan gave to his children a religion soaked in gloom and marveled at the irreligious young people. We now understand that religion is first of all to live by, and that the gospel is good news to boys and girls when given to them in a large sympathy with the abounding life of youth.

## 3. *To Enforce Correct Belief*

The early instruction of children by the church was through the catechism. Great care was taken in the formulation of the doctrines of the church by great councils who ordered that their ponderous and letter-perfect definitions be imposed on the memories of little children. It was an effective scheme to rob youth of intellectual liberty and maintain the infallibility of the church. The Protestant spirit challenges any attempt to cast truth into a final statement and insists that education free the soul of man. In their zeal for a form of truth dear to their own hearts some churches are ordering that Sunday-school instruction confine itself to a creed which they have prescribed. This attempt always defeats itself.

### 4. To Make the Bible Familiar

The Reformation threw off the authority of an infallible church and found the authority for the church in a divine book. With the retirement of the catechetical method of teaching, Sunday-school lessons have been based on the Bible. The International Sunday School Lesson Committee has wielded a mighty influence in the United States and Canada, and its reiterated purpose is to secure a familiarity with all parts of the Bible. " Thy word is a lamp unto my feet and a guide to my path."

We have found from experience that correct information even of the Bible does not secure correct conduct. An essential part of the work of religious education is to pass the knowledge of the truth into the practise of the truth. If the age-old truth is to be lived under changed conditions of life, some study must be made of the world today, especially as determining forms of service.

### 5. To Teach the Child

Educational theory has swung away from a book-made curriculum to a first emphasis on the child. A restudy of

the method of Jesus discovers that long before Pestalozzi
the Master Teacher placed the child in the midst. We now
understand that the school is not organized for the schoolmaster or the teacher, though some of them still think
so, but it is organized for the pupil. But this statement
of aim is too vague and too partial. Our teaching is for
the individual, and also for society, as we shall see.

### 6. To Produce Useful Church-members

A natural and proper expectation is that those who are
instructed by the church shall become members of the
church. It would be a strange plan of church training
which failed to consider the needs of the church of the
future and had no responsibility for providing intelligent
and devoted members of the church. But church-membership does not exhaust all the relationships and possibilities
of a human life. Our aim in religious education must be
as big as life itself. We must expect to make efficient
church-members and also give help to all life's normal
relations.

### 7. To Secure Social Efficiency

Christ had much to say about a wonderful social organization which he called the Kingdom of God, or of
Heaven. Living in a democratic organization of government and society has taught us that the ideas and practises
of individual citizens create the state. The church must
be concerned for social well-being. It cannot but be concerned for grave social evils. The church must include
a social message in its instruction. While this aim is
not sufficient by itself, it must be made a part of our final
statement of aim.

### 8. *To Strengthen a Missionary Enterprise*

William Carey and Adoniram Judson and their fellow pioneers began a new era for the church. A comfortable church must not be permitted to settle down selfishly at ease at home. It must be concerned for the unevangelized in all the dark corners of the wide world. Youth will bear a significant part in this daring enterprise. An important element of religious education is missionary education. It is imperative that the church make more and more effective its missionary training. But we must beware lest enthusiastic souls persuade the church that missionary work is the exclusive purpose of all its training.

## Factors in Our Ultimate Aim

It is not possible at this stage to formulate a final statement of our complete aim in religious education. Further investigation and experimentation and discussion must be carried on before we can reach a statement which will be generally accepted. We can make the distinction between ultimate aim and immediate aims. We can note that immediate aims have to do with age groups, beginning with the major divisions of childhood, youth, and adults. Specialists in the education of each of these groups are attempting to state their particular aims. We can state the factors which must enter the final statement of our ultimate aim.

Our aim in religious education must define:

### 1. *What We Are Seeking to Do for the Individual Pupil*

We begin with a simple acquaintance with God, such as a child may have. As Jesus taught us, we make use of the personal relationships of the home to make real the care and love of the Unseen Father.

After the child has learned of Jesus as friend we expect to make him known as Saviour. From him we come to know the Life Beautiful and the awakening of conscience. A painful sense of falling short of his loving demands becomes repentance. He graciously reveals himself as our Saviour from sin.

We expect to assist the young disciple to know and live his truth. Life is in the making and must pass through a succession of adjustments and readjustments. Ideals must be constructed. Habits must be formed. Attitudes must be established. Skills must be developed. Right motives for all this varied experience will flow from relationship to Christ.

We aim to help toward a life of fruitful and happy service. We should train in the stewardship of time, money, and life. We should make known world conditions which call for service. We must make compelling Christ's principle of a sacrificial life.

## 2. What We Are Seeking to Do for the Church

Through the religious education of the youth of today we are building the church of tomorrow. We are seeking to encourage group loyalties as a preparation for church loyalties. We are forming a church consciousness through studying and playing and working together. We aim to exalt the idea of the church by training imagination and aspiration to see the church as it is in the mind of Christ, the ideal church. An important part of the service which religious education renders the future church is the training of leaders. Our aim must include a course of training in principles and practise, for the preparation of workers at home and abroad.

## 3. What We Are Seeking to Do for the Community

Religion should reach into all human relationships—school life, business life, social life, professional life, recreational life, political life. The school, and particularly the school of the church is dealing with those moral and religious values which directly affect the community. The church seeks to bring in the Kingdom of God by teaching the truth of God. The community has much to give the church—its good-will, the maintenance of law and public order, the protection of its property and its rights. The church also has much to give the immediate and the distant community.

## A Tentative Statement of Aim

It will be necessary for church leadership to formulate a working statement of its aim in religious education. It will not be possible to proceed with the work of organizing the forces of the church and outlining a program until some agreement is reached on what it is all about. Even if it is not possible to make a formal and all-inclusive statement which will be satisfactory to all, some attempt must be made in this direction for the sake of progress. Probably more than one meeting of the responsible leaders in the educational work of the church will debate various statements of aim seeking compactness and comprehensiveness. With many misgivings the following statement is made, not in any sense as a final statement, but as a help to those who are seeking to unify many unrelated agencies and activities.

> *The Christian church should seek through religious education to bring all the experiences of childhood, youth, and adulthood under the control of the ideals of the living Christ in order to Christianize motives, attitudes, habits, skills, conduct, relationships, and ideals for the enrichment of the individual, the strengthening of every worthy social institution, including the church, and the extension of the Kingdom of God among all peoples.*

This definition of aim grades our task and reminds us we must adapt our work to age groups. It emphasizes the element of control for the immature and unorganized, not that life may be suppressed but made consistent with itself and infinitely enriched. It calls attention to the teachableness of the religion of Jesus, since he came teaching us an ideal of life, an ideal which he completely fills as the living Christ. No religious education is worthy the name which does not achieve the difficult feat of reaching beyond information and activity to motive. Attitude as a composite of deep and abiding emotion and equally deep and abiding conviction is a determining factor in character. Many times we omit the discovery and development of skills and overlook the significance of all social relationships, but they are needed in building a Kingdom of Heaven. This statement includes evangelism as that process which brings the individual under the control of the living Christ. Missionary education is made imperative by the necessity of extending the Kingdom of God among all peoples.

## Help for the Teacher

If the church is to face its teaching responsibility it must first of all seek to define its aim. It becomes apparent (1) that the church must teach certain subjects for a certain purpose, (2) under a comprehensive plan that will include organization, study, leadership, and equipment. (3) A help to a statement of aim is found in the historical study of past educational aims, (4) and of contemporary educational influences, (5) together with a study of past aims in religious education. (6) This will lead us to list the factors that must enter into a present statement of aim and (7) the formulation of a working aim.

## Questions for Further Study

1. Secure from all the leaders in your church a statement of their educational aim.

2. Formulate for yourself a statement of what should be the aim in religious education.

3. Applying the suggested factors in aim to the different age groups, state what should be the religious education aim in dealing with the primary child, junior, intermediate, senior, young people, and adult.

# MEANS OF ACHIEVING THE AIM OF THE CHURCH

You may take ever so careful an aim, but if the gun is not loaded all your effort is useless. Having considered the essential factors which must enter into an adequate aim for religious education we are now compelled to ask: How can we realize our aim? What means are available for attaining the objectives as stated in the aim? We will now consider the various agencies and influences which have been operating in the field of religious education, examine their values and inquire whether they may be so related to each other as to form something of a unified system of education.

## Home Training Has First Place

Ruskin wrote of his mother:

She established my soul in life. And truly though I have picked up the elements of a little further knowledge this maternal installation of my mind (through memorizing Bible passages) I count very confidently the most precious and on the whole, the one essential part of my education.

The home is so tremendously significant in shaping character because in early life it is the only influence reaching the growing child. It surrounds the child at the period when imitation is at its highest. The home influences are intensified by the intimacy of family life, deepened through an appreciation of the ties of kinship and the growth of

48

affection. The private life of parents, of older relatives included in the home circle, and of older brothers and sisters, serve as examples to the younger children, all the more powerful because of the close contacts. XThe ideals of the home, as determined largely by the parents and expressing themselves in a thousand different ways, are daily operative in fixing character. This makes the home preeminent in moral and religious training. Probably it is not too much to say that the average man or woman does not rise above the level established in the early home. In the home of a winsome religious life and a firm, gentle moral discipline children begin life with a great advantage over those whose homes are irreligious and lacking in careful character training. Some way must be found to help homes which are neglecting their important share in the religious education of the child.

## The Community Influences the Child

In this day of multiplied and complex social relationships it is as impossible for a family to separate itself from the community as it is for the individual to exist as a hermit. Modern life makes us dependent upon each other. Families learn that they need neighbors when crises arise, if they have not discovered it before.

The child is adventurous and sociable. He wants to explore beyond his own dooryard. Above all, he craves society of his kind. Mother and the adult members of the family may seek to be all the child's society, but in vain. A mighty impulse is thrusting him forth to seek playfellows. Through these children of other homes new influences begin their long work in the changing child. The community is claiming him.

The community of childhood is extended and organized in the common school. A new world opens to solicit little feet. The spirit of the community expresses itself in the orderly government and adult leadership of the school, but much more in the standards, sentiments, prejudices, and practises established in the boy world and in the girl world. If we are concerned for the shaping of this plastic bit of humanity we must be interested in the ideals forming in the community of childhood.

Community influences are operative in both country and city. On the farm, especially in the thinly settled regions, families see less of each other than in the more compact settlement, but even in the country modern conditions tend to draw folks together by the telephone, good roads, and the automobile, a neighborhood shopping center, cooperative business arrangements, the social life of the Grange, county fairs, institutes for farmers and farm women, boys' corn clubs and pig clubs, and many another community enterprise. Inevitably the children and young people are drawn under community influences.

Especially significant in their effect upon young people are the amusements created or permitted by the community. Love of a good time is not to be condemned as of the devil, for it belongs by right to the normal life of the adolescent. Amusements are of two kinds: (1) Those created by the activity of the young people themselves, and (2) those which provide diversion through the performances of other people. The former give opportunity for the wholesome development of the physical, intellectual, and social life. The latter make possible professionalism and commercialism. The determination of standards for both forms of amusement rests with the community.

The organization of the economic life of the community affects everybody. There is no question more fundamental than the bread-and-butter question. A people living on the rim of poverty and under the shadow of threatening starvation, are necessarily limited in their culture, refinements, enjoyment of life and spiritual resources. All of the community must be interested in the business of the community but must not be so absorbed in the material gains of business as to be blind to the evil influences of an unjust economic order. The same is true of the political order. We are bound together into a political unit as inevitably as we are made one economically. The standards of our politics have a wide-reaching influence on youth. No matter how much we would prefer a simple life untrammeled by social obligations, for better or worse we are tied up in a great social order. No scheme of education can be without concern for the moral and religious influences of that social order.

## The Church Extends a Pastoral Care

On one occasion Jesus is reported by Matthew to have looked out upon the multitude as sheep without a shepherd and was touched with compassion. It was an earnest concern of the Master to reach out an unsolicited pastoral care to young and old. This is his purpose in founding and maintaining his church.

In the name of the heavenly Father the church seeks to bestow blessing and care upon all within its influence. It is interested in every community agency which is helping folks. It is concerned for a wholesome family life which gives every child a preparation for the highest and best. It is concerned for a thorough-going public-school training which reaches all the children of all the people. It is concerned for the amusement and recreational opportunities and standards of the community. It is concerned about economic and political conditions. It is concerned for public morals, just legislation, and the impartial enforcement of law.

In addition to all this social concern, a concern that other agencies serve the community faithfully, the church is also concerned to perform conscientiously a task committed exclusively to it. A definite responsibility for religious education belongs to the church and cannot be delegated to any other agency. Before the parents bring their child to the church and place him under the pastoral care of the church, provision for the child's training through life ought to be thought through and set up in a definite plan. The educational plan of the church should be: (1) Comprehensive. It should aim to develop symmetrically all sides of the growing life. (2) Continuing. It should expect to claim the attendance of the child and man throughout the whole life. (3) Human. It will remember that folks are just folks, that a paper plan may look good but actually be inhuman, and that the demand for patience and faith in boys and girls will never cease. (4) Generous. It should give and give again of money, time, thought, and all that life holds dear.

### The Church Has a Primary Concern in Evangelism

When a church stands between the soul and God mediating as a priest, it attempts what it cannot perform. The Church of the Reformation in seeking to be true to the New Testament, disclaims any priestly functions but faithfully points the soul to our only Great High Priest. Before all things else the church must not encourage any one old or young to depend upon it for eternal life, but must insistently present Jesus Christ as the Shepherd and Bishop of our souls.

Little children must be taught that Jesus is their Shepherd true. They will readily grasp the relationship between the shepherd and his sheep, sense his care for the weak little lambs, and easily transfer the teaching to Jesus and themselves. From the earliest contacts in the Cradle Roll class through the elementary division, instruction and worship and prayer and song should build up a recognition and understanding of the personal relationship of each little life to the Saviour. In their childish way they will come to know his desire for their affection and simple trust, and they will respond to his love.

Mrs. Lamoreaux writes in " The Pupils in the Church School " as follows:

If the atmosphere of the home is vital and warm with Christian influences a child may never know any time when he did not love Jesus Christ and want to obey him. Sometimes a child reaches a period of clearer understanding of what is involved in obedience to Christ before he considers his own personal relation to him and consciously takes him as his King and Leader. Sometimes life has been lived for many years contrary to the spirit and will of Christ, and in penitence and surrender one must receive him as Saviour and Lord. But however or whenever it may come to pass, Jesus Christ must be consciously, willingly, and genuinely enthroned as the Saviour and Master of life if it is to reach its highest development.[1]

Part of the task of the church in religious education is to train teachers to win souls. They should know with some clearness the way of salvation, and be impelled

[1] Copyright, 1927, by The Judson Press.

by so friendly a yearning that they will not be satisfied until every member of the class has been won to an intelligent acceptance and open confession of Christ.

A Sunday-school teacher in an Illinois town had an unusually shy boy in her intermediate class. Whenever she called at the front door of his home he would flee through the back door. By chance she learned of his interest in chickens. She sent to the Government bureau in Washington for pamphlets on the care of chickens, their feeding, housing, breeding, varieties, etc. After cramming chicken knowledge she called on her boy, but not at the front door. She found her way to the back door and caught him on the fly. Tactfully she managed to secure an invitation to see his chickens. To his surprise her questions revealed a knowledge that amazed and disarmed him. His shyness disappeared, and in that chicken-yard was formed the beginnings of a friendship that was to lead him to Christ as his Saviour.

The church-school leadership must be concerned to sound the evangelistic note in the devotional services of the departments, insist upon lesson study material with evangelistic emphasis, encourage teachers to become soul-winners and follow some careful plan of securing public confession, training for church-membership, and entrance into the church.

## Religious Character Is Developed by Worship

The impulse to worship is found among all races and in all ages. When Paul on Mars Hill called attention to the altar to the Unseen God he pointed to a hunger of the human heart everywhere. This native impulse has mighty possibilities of good and of evil. Without guidance it is uninformed, productive of fantastic ceremonies, superstitious, enslaving and debasing.

Jesus' example is significant as to public and private worship. He attended the synagogue service of his boyhood training as long as the rulers of the synagogue permitted. Up to the very last he gathered with his people in the Temple at the great Passover festival. All of the Gospel writers note the prominent place which solitary prayer had in his busy life.

On the quiet Sunday morning in the country the churchbell carries far its sweet appealing note. That bell voices the need of human lives and also the imperative call of the Ineffable Majesty, " Thou shalt worship the Lord thy God." It is the business of the church to carry home to every responsible moral being within reach the summons to worship and also to give the immature and ignorant training in worship.

It is expected that the church will provide public services of worship for the community. Public worship should be : (1) Appealing. It must be full of life and earnestness and sense of reality. It must never degenerate to mere entertainment. (2) Uplifting. It is designed to draw all worshipers into a unity of thought and feeling, and lift all into the august, purifying, loving Presence. (3) Habitual. It aims to establish faithfulness in attendance irrespective of passing whims or fickle weather. (4) Reverent. It is fitting that lowly creatures approach the mysterious sanctuary in awe and contrition. (5) Sincere. A subtle danger in an oft-repeated form is that it may become mere lip service. They that worship the Father must worship him in spirit and truth, for such he seeketh to worship him.

E

The Lord gave us one form of prayer, but he did not indicate any form of worship. In addition to public worship two forms have established themselves in Christian practise: (1) Family worship. It is meet that all the members of the home gather regularly to recognize Jehovah and all his goodness to them. Such a service lifts the whole tone of family life. The church may help the home maintain the family altar. (2) Private worship. " Enter into thy closet, and when thou hast shut the door, pray to thy Father which seeth in secret, and he will reward thee openly." Early in life and throughout life the practise of private prayer needs to be cultivated.

Training in worship is now recognized as an essential part of religious education. Growing life should pass through a deepening experience in worship. Group worship requires: (1) Prepared leaders. It is unfortunate when a group in training is handled by a haphazard leadership which has rushed into this holy service without preparation. Leaders need an understanding of the nature of worship, need a prepared heart and a carefully considered program for each occasion. (2) Materials of worship. Books are needed containing appropriate responses and helpful music. An instrument in good tune is a help. (3) Suitable building. A service which depends upon its emotional impressiveness is greatly influenced by the physical environment. The room should suggest the mystery and detachment of worship and assist the mind to enter into the deep significances of Christian worship.

## Preaching Builds Christian Character

Worship and preaching have long been associated. When Jesus went into the synagogue at Nazareth to worship they handed him the scroll of Isaiah the prophet, and he began to expound the Scriptures. In Protestant practise the service of worship has usually been connected with a service of preaching. We have seen that the justification for this is the command of the Lord.

The preacher is an expositor. He is a student of the Scriptures. He has been trained to divide rightly the word of truth. He seeks to make plain the way of holiness so that " wayfaring men, yea, fools, shall not err therein." Such is the living power of the old Book that faithful expository preaching arrests attention, arouses the conscience, and opens new meanings to life.

The preacher is a prophet. He speaks for God. He is the living messenger of the living God to living men. His function is not merely the expounding of a literature of the past. He has been called to the gospel ministry for such times as these. His association with men and women and boys and girls, and his study of his own times give him a present-day message. Every interest and need of the religious life is a live pulpit theme.

The influence of preaching on Christian living is summarized by Paul in his charge to the young preacher Timothy: " I solemnly implore you in the presence of God and of Christ Jesus, who is about to judge the living and the dead, proclaim God's message, be zealous in season and out of season; convince, rebuke, encourage, with the utmost patience as a teacher " (*Weymouth's Translation*).

## The Church Community Is a Great Educational Institution

A good high school or college is something more than classrooms, lesson courses, laboratories, faculty, gymnasium, equipment. It is a great institution separating a group of selected folks into an intense community life which stimulates, modifies, develops its members in un-numbered ways. Similarly a live church is something more than its preaching and teaching and service. The church creates a community of chosen people within the community. The church community is constantly influenc-ing its constituency in a thousand ways, as by-products of its central purpose to ennoble life.

The advantages of the church as an educational institu-tion have been summarized by Doctor Cope in " Religious Education in the Church " :

First, it has an advantage as a society. Modern education seeks to provide natural social relations and conditions which the life of the church supplies. Second, the church has the advantage of indirection. The educational process goes forward largely uncon-sciously. The institution is not labelled a school. Third, it has the advantage of ideal aims. Fourth, its work furnishes ample opportunity for activities which are commonly simple outgrowths of the social relationships and the high ideals. Fifth, the greater part of instruction may be closely related to experience. Sixth, it reaches all kinds of persons all through their lives.[2]

## Courses of Study Are an Important Factor in Christian Training

Christianity is the religion of a person. In making known that great personality a great book plays a leading part. The Bible is not only the great charter of the faith, but by reason of its popular character it is the text-book of the people. It has been written not for an esoteric circle of savants and priests but for the common man. Protestantism has built great publishing societies, translat-

[2] Used by permission of Charles Scribner's Sons, owners of copyright.

ing the text into the vernacular of every race and every tribe with a written language. Indeed, such is the anxiety of the missionary spirit of the church to cause every man to hear and read in his own tongue, primitive spoken languages have been reduced to written symbols in order to give the Bible to the people.

It is important to note that the Bible has material of interest to children, youth, and adults. Little children need the help of an informed mother or teacher in finding what is there for them, but it is there. Young people familiar with school text-books will be greatly helped by a Bible text-book which organizes the Scripture material in a way they can most readily use. Even adults, and especially those lacking in special training, will find Bible study most profitable when some helps are supplied. The editor of Bible text material is sometimes forgotten by the churches, but he is rendering a service of inestimable value. His is the service of opening to a clearer understanding a book which is inherently interesting to all life.

Marked advance has been made in improving Bible text-books. The new emphasis in Sunday-school work, placing the child first, has wrought mighty changes in the form and content of lesson material. It now seeks to attract and hold the attention of the pupil. It is no longer a little book of sermonettes for the preacher-teacher. It approaches the study of the Bible from the interest and need of the child, and expects to present lesson material in such form that the pupil can master it.

Vacation schools and week-day schools have demanded text-books adapted to their specialized need. For the Vacation school a variety of graded material has been necessary to fit into the unique Vacation-school program.

It must include story material, helps for handwork, and a rich choice of expressional work, musical material, devotional helps, and many suggestions how to vary the program for restless youngsters during hot summer days in the crowded city. The Week-day school text-book is in the process of development through the work of many experimenters. Unlike the Vacation-school text it must be a pupil book. There will be teachers' helps, but it must give material to be set before the pupil for his conquest. It must reach the level of the public-school text-books.

Study-books must be prepared on material other than Biblical. From a growing group of writers we have text-books on missions, on stewardship, on leadership training, on church history, on church efficiency, on Christian ethics, on Christian doctrine, on social problems, etc. The committee on curriculum for the church school has now a rich variety for selection.

## The Church Is Interested in Social Life

What is it that makes a boy wash his neck and behind his ears, spend unconscionable time before the mirror plastering to smoothness his unruly hair, and adjusting to a nicety his gay new necktie? That same boy was the despair of his mother but a few months before because he refused to take any concern for his personal appearance. The reason every man knows, yes, and woman too. The social impulse has been born. Henceforth youth must know a growing hunger for the society of his kind and will be very much perturbed if anything serves as a barrier to social acceptance.

Nature introduces one of the strongest character-forming influences with the coming of desired associates. The group of young people that adopts him can make such changes in him that his mother will hardly recognize him as the same boy. Even one outstanding character who has attained group leadership can work revolutionary changes in moral ideals and practises. Such is the power of good and evil associates.

In every circle of young people amusements play a large part. "Let's go," said the impatient young soldier. Restless youth is constantly saying, "Let's go." Not more ceaseless and steady is the spring's flow than the flow of nervous energy through young brains and hands and feet. It matters a great deal whether the forms of recreation are sound and wholesome. It is a serious concern of the future if groups of young women and young men can find no better place for the exchanges of social life than a dance-hall. On the other hand, play in the open amid good surroundings and governed by impartial rules and high standards of mutual respect makes the recreational life a means to lofty character.

The church itself needs sociability. It is impossible for any church to do its proper work in an absence of acquaintance and friendliness. Means must be found of bringing the membership together under pleasant circumstances for the cultivation of comradeship and church loyalty. Sad is the condition of a church which has divided into separate social sets, which is snobbish and uninterested in strangers, and which impresses the newcomer as cold and unsociable. In such a depressing atmosphere spiritual results are almost impossible.

Those who are responsible for the program of religious education in the church must consider the needs of sociability and of recreation. Because of the marked influence on the individual and on the church life we need a church program of recreation.

## Christian Character Includes Service and Sacrifice

"He that saveth his life shall lose it, and he that loseth his life for my sake and the gospel's shall save it." In these words Jesus states his ideal for the Christian. He is not to live for himself, but for others. He must find some means of overcoming the strong desire of nature toward selfishness and develop the habit of service.

Long before modern pedagogy made the discovery, Jesus taught that we learn by doing. "You cannot understand the motive which caused me to wash your feet, Peter," he said, "until you perform menial services for those who misunderstand you and are unworthy such services." In the religion of Jesus peculiarly, its inner spirit can only be understood by those who practise his precepts.

The church must accompany the preaching of the Cross by a presentation of need which will call forth a ministry of service. Those who have been touched by His spirit will respond when they know there is a man fallen by the roadside and neeeding the personal services of a good Samaritan. Training for service must include information as to the need of service. The church must make a world survey of need in the light of the Great Commission and an equally faithful survey of need in its immediate community. Help must be given untrained folks to find the places that need them.

Every group which has undertaken some part of religious education must have its program of service. It is not enough to have a program of recreational activities. Some group appeal should be made for unselfish service in the name of the Christ. This will be possible if the church itself has a worthy program of service. Fundamental in such a program will be the training and practise of Christian stewardship.

## A Unified Aim Requires a Unified Organization

In our study of the aim in religious education we have seen that the unity of human life compels us to seek a unified statement of aim. It is not sufficient that a number of organizations within the church like the Sunday school and the Young People's Society and the Woman's Missionary Society have aims for themselves, it is essential that we have an all-inclusive church aim.

The past efforts of the church have been haphazard largely because we left to separate groups the determination of what they would do with a segment of a human life. We have seen how these organizations fail to reenforce and supplement each other, how they overlap, and how frequently friction and competition are developed.

We must face the urgent demand for one organization to realize our single aim. We must secure a church leadership larger than any group leadership, and begin to build an adequate church organization for religious education. This leadership will be made responsible for a uniform administration of grading, for the selection of graded study courses, for a general plan of leadership training, pupil participation, and all the elements of a church program.

The ordinary method of building a church organization for religious education will be through correlation to unification. Because of old loyalties and habits of thinking and working, it will not be possible in the average church to secure a unified scheme immediately. We must study how to bring about correlation or cooperation of our present agencies and leadership, then we can advance as rapidly as seems wise toward unification. There are possibilities of holding our folks through all the periods of growing life, and possibilities of enriching these periods beyond all that we are now doing if we can attain to a real church organization for religious education.

## Our Supreme Emphasis Must Be Spiritual

There is a subtle danger in all school work. We are likely to turn education into routine. Our educational leaders are saying so much about new methods and forms of organization and material that we may easily become lost in the mechanics. Religious education may become for us an intellectual diversion engaged in bandying terms, or a scheme of socialization which has dropped all religious content. Let us remember that this is all the work of One greater than we, and that all our *busyness* and feverish activity can accomplish nothing of value except as he gives spiritual life and fruitage. Let us stop ever and anon to test our work for spiritual results.

## Help for the Teacher

If the church is to teach it must of necessity employ certain agencies in teaching. The purpose of this chapter is to list the principal means the church is using or should use; to look briefly at each one, and thus get a bird's-eye view of the whole task before becoming absorbed in a detailed study. It will afford the teacher an opportunity to enlarge upon any point which may have particular local application but for which there has n<u>ot</u> been room for full development in this book.

## Topics for Further Study

1. Write to denominational headquarters for description of lesson courses and sample lessons.

2. List the means of religious education employed by your own church.

3. Read and report on "Religious Education in the Church," Henry F. Cope. Scribner's, 1918.

# V

## BUILDING A CURRICULUM

In a family of several children distributed through high school and entering college, many arguments arose. Very frequently the debate turned on the meaning of terms. The family slogan came to be, " Go to Uncle Dick." The big dictionary was kept conveniently near, and excited disputants were referred to his impartial court.

The term " curriculum " is not altogether clear, so we will go to the dictionary and to the ancient language whose word we have borrowed for our modern tongue.

### Derivation and Definition

" Curriculum " is a Latin word meaning " a running, course, race," from the verb *curro,* run. The Century Dictionary defines our use of the word in modern English, " A course, specifically a fixed course of study in a university, college, or school, as, the curriculum of arts; the medical curriculum." This definition would make curriculum mean the sum of lesson materials to be taught. President W. A. Harper [1] broadens this definition as he applies it to religious education, " We may define the curriculum as the sum total of those educational influences that enter into the direction and formation of Christian character." Professor G. A. Coe [2] writes, " We are coming to see that the curriculum is to be neither study nor the

[1] " An Integrated Program of Religious Education." Quoted by permission of the Macmillan Company, owner of copyright.
[2] " Social Theory of Religious Education." Quoted by permission of Charles Scribner's Sons, owners of copyright.

66

subject-matter to be studied, but rather it is to be the process of living in such a way that one grows normally into the power and habit and the disposition to live in a right way."

## Origins

From the above definitions it is evident that the curriculum includes all the subject-matter of education, and that the organizing of the curriculum is one of the big tasks of the school leadership. Where did the materials of our present curriculum come from? Perhaps an understanding of the origin of these materials will suggest how we can organize our present wealth of material.

Let us use a common illustration of the origin of teaching materials. The Indian depended upon his hunting skill for the family food supply. He was therefore interested in the wild animals whose flesh was serviceable for food. He studied their habits, disposition, haunts, physical strength, and endurance. He practised his own skill in tracking, in trapping, and in attack with weapons. He trained himself to undergo physical strain, cultivated his powers of eye and ear, and developed mental alertness. All this information and skill and his ideal of a great hunter he sought to give to his boy. The Indian's curriculum came out of experience and was selected for its use in controlling experience.

When life is primitive and simple it is not necessary to organize a separate school and set up a formal curriculum. Instruction is woven into every-day experience. The young Indian becomes a hunter by listening to the tales about the camp-fire, by his play with bow and arrow, by accompanying hunters as a menial helper with his imita-

tive powers sharply alert, and then on his own. His training as a hunter continues as long as he practises hunting.
The conditions of his life furnish the motives for learning
and supply him with the means of acquiring the information and skill he knows that he needs. Similarly he is introduced to the ideals and mysteries of the tribe.

As man progressed toward higher levels of civilization
he accumulated larger knowledge of the world in which
he lived, a more varied skill as a workman, and more
elaborate ideals of individual and social life. All of this
material developed out of his experience and was valuable
for guiding experience. This material grew to such proportions that it became impossible for any boy to acquire it
all, or even the part which would be significant for him,
without special help. It was also true that valuable knowledge was in danger of becoming lost through lack of
proper care in preservation and transmission. The educational function of the family and of the tribe was gathered
into the school and the professional teacher and the organized curriculum.

This brief study of the origins of our formal curriculum
makes it plain that apart from experience it has no meaning, but that its test must always be the degree to which it
functions in experience. We are too much inclined to
think of curriculum as a body of knowledge, whereas it
must include skills, habits, virtues, and ideals. Professor
Irving E. Miller says: [3]

There are habits of personal bearing, of promptness, of neatness, of accuracy that have a definite social value. The virtues of
courage, of patience, of persistence, of regard for the rights of

---

[3] " Education for the Needs of Life." Quoted by permission of the author
and of the Macmillan Company, publishers.

others, of obedience, of self-reliance are all things to be inculcated. They belong in the curriculum of instruction, whether specified or not. So it is with the great ideals, such as those of religious toleration, freedom of thought, democracy, individual rights, social justice. These ideals have not been attained without bloody struggle in the past. It would be a crime against posterity to let them disintegrate and die out. They represent fundamental social values of greater importance than the knowledge of a vocation or the preservation of any specific kind of knowledge.

## History

No question before educators today is more confusing than the question of the curriculum. No factor in our educational scheme arouses more criticism. An increasing number of writers predict that it will be the chief problem under consideration for years to come. As a help toward a better understanding of the questions at issue it would be well to review the modern theories of the curriculum which are still influential.

### *1. The Theory of the Curriculum as Discipline*

The feudal society of the Middle Ages emphasized authority and unquestioning obedience. It is not surprising that the current philosophy of education made the schoolmaster an absolute monarch who considered his curriculum chiefly as a means of discipline. The value of an education did not consist in the worthfulness of the subjects learned but in the difficult process of learning. The subjects most difficult and most disliked by the student possessed maximum value as disciplinary studies. This era made large use of the motto, " Spare the rod and spoil the child." The disciplinary theory has been discounted because it was built on a faulty psychology. A better understanding of the mind as a unity and of the possibility of enlisting the child's interest in his own education is working the change.

## 2. The Theory of the Curriculum as Knowledge

This theory is one of the oldest in practise, though its formulation awaited the genius of Herbart. A large share of the content of the curriculum is the body of knowledge which has been gathered by the generations. Before written language this knowledge was communicated orally. With the advent of writing, and especially of printing, this knowledge was committed to text-books adapted to the business of instruction. The conception of the curriculum as a series of text-books containing valuable knowledge easily became established and still holds large place.

This theory regards the pupil as largely a passive agent. A better psychology has made the learner the active, selecting, appropriating agent. It has been discovered that even a glib memoriter recitation does not prove that the pupil has mastered the material. Life calls for the dynamic spirit, creative, responsible, pioneering. An exclusive attention to the knowledge of the past will chain one's spirit to the past to the neglect of the future. Knowledge cannot be an end in itself but is valuable only as it serves the purposes of a creative spirit.

## 3. The Theory of the Curriculum as Means to Enriched and Controlled Experience

The emphasis has shifted from the material and process to personality. We are now interested in the growth of personality which we have discovered is dynamic, self-organizing, and self-controlling. It is reaching through a controlled experience toward self-realization. Moreover, we find that active personality is shaping itself in partnership with other active personalities in a changing society. The curriculum must give assistance to individual character in the process of becoming, and to a developing social order.

The curriculum must serve to enrich experience. It will explain and interpret experience, making plain its significance for the individual and for his associates, and give the experience a depth and reach. The curriculum will assist the pupil to control his experience by defining the ends he seeks, organizing their values, and bringing his experiences under the control of a dominant purpose.

On Saturday morning mother takes daughter into the kitchen to teach her to cook. In this laboratory of domestic science the pupil has at hand her materials and tools and her instructor who carries the curriculum in her hand in the shape of a book of recipes and in her head in the shape of practical wisdom. If the disciplinary theory of the curriculum obtained, a stern mother would drag an unwilling daughter through a distasteful procedure without any effort to win her interest and in the hope that she was developing a faculty—say, a faculty for construction. If the knowledge theory of the curriculum holds sway, mother becomes a pedagogue interested in transmitting through five formal steps an organized body of knowledge to a passive pupil who may sit with folded hands. If the enriched and controlled experience theory is operative, mother is most interested in her daughter's activity of mind and hand that through that activity definite gains may be secured in baking a cake for the afternoon party, and in making a good cook, helpful to many people.

F

## The Troubled Situation in General Education

It is a notorious fact that the school tends to dig a rut for itself by the practise of a formal and unnatural method of teaching which separates it from life. The public school in America is charged with this tendency by outspoken critics who are among our leading educators and sincere friends of the school. It is affirmed by convention speakers and text-book writers that the curriculum of the public school is overcrowded with courses, that studies are isolated from one another and from life, that studies are being condensed into dull generalities, that time is wasted on trivial and miscellaneous topics, that the curriculum is static with factual material, that it is a system of wearisome repetitions from grade to grade, and most seriously that it is an obsolete plan of organization into separate, unrelated individual studies.

An earnest search is being made by many public-school leaders for a better method of organizing the school curriculum. It is plain that a purpose of the school is to relate the pupil to the outer world of nature and human society. The outer world has the right to impose its laws on the child. The pathway to freedom and the control of nature for the child lies through obedience. The curriculum is the means by which the child and the world are brought into an understanding and agreement. There is an organized knowledge which the child is bound to respect, come to terms with, and by some means conquer. Professor Charles A. McMurry points out two phases of this relationship with which the curriculum is concerned: (1) The outside world of nature and human society is the sphere where education must register its results. If the pupil leaves school to wander aimless and unrelated to actual life, the school suffers indictment. (2) The child has strong ties of kinship with the world and a vital connection with the life of the community. The school is at fault if it builds a curriculum and ignores these many potential motives for learning.

## The Project Method in Curriculum Building

The conviction is gaining ground that our present arrangement of studies is lacking in unity, does not awaken the desire to learn as it ought, and detaches the pupil from the community life. Numbers of investigators and experimenters have been making their own studies of the child's natural method of learning and have made tentative ventures toward the reorganization of the school curriculum. A strong movement has developed in the direction of project material. Miss Margaret E. Wells teaching in a Trenton, New Jersey, school found that a day early in the fall term was given to the children to attend the State Fair with tickets gratuitously provided. The three grades under her charge were so excited over what they saw and heard and had so many questions to ask, that she drew from them the suggestion to make a fair of their own. For many weeks they were busy making exhibits and amusement features to which parents were to be invited. As they were " Playing Fair " during the weeks, they acquired arithmetic, spelling, geography, reading, writing, etc., which they hardly recognized under these formal names. When that project came to a natural end others were found: " Playing City," " Playing Store," " Playing Families." This is just a sample of what many have been attempting. Miss Wells has formulated some curriculum principles based on her project experiment: "Nature's motive power, the play spirit, should furnish the drives for children's activities." "Through play the child should be led to habits of happy, useful work." "All of the native equipment of the child should be utilized." "The necessities common to children in all localities should determine the general framework of the curriculum, details being fixed by the varying conditions of environment." "The so-called subjects of the curriculum should be taught as interrelated phases of life, the psychological rather than the logical order being followed in teaching." "Abundant opportunity should be provided for such doing as shall stimulate thinking and thus lead to further doing and thinking." "Group consciousness and group sympathies should be developed through group activities." [4]

## The Troubled Situation in Religious Education

The curriculum now in use in the average church school is very unsatisfactory. It has been thrown together without any principle of organization. It is composed of a variety of material issuing from unrelated sources and constructed according to many theories of the curriculum, not always harmonious. In a great number of churches it can hardly be called a curriculum in the sense of constituting a system of studies and activities.

The Sunday-school cause has been served by a curriculum committee for more than fifty years. It is a notable instance of a continuing and effective interdenominational service, and testifies to the strength of the move-

[4] The above quotations, taken from "A Project Curriculum," by Margaret Elizabeth Wells, are used by permission of the author and her publisher, J. B. Lippincott Company.

ment for religious education and to the strong ties binding together the evangelical churches. Ever since the memorable Indianapolis Convention of the International Sunday School Association in 1872 the International Lesson Committee has been preparing lesson outlines. Beginning with the Uniform Lessons which undertook to cover the entire Bible by a single lesson each Sunday for old and young in a cycle of seven years (later changed to six years), the Committee modified the plan in 1918 by issuing the Improved Uniform Lessons. This system uses a different lesson title and offers an adapted treatment in the lessons for the earlier grades. The International Convention at Louisville in 1908 voted to instruct the Lesson Committee to issue a Graded Series. This became known as the Closely Graded Series. It consists of seventeen units graded one unit to each year from the age of four to twenty. It comprises two sets of text-books for each year, one for the pupil and one for the teacher, published in parts, four to the year, or one hundred thirty-six parts. The Committee has later organized a Group Graded Series which advance not by one-year steps as in the Closely Graded but by three-year steps. Several publishers have provided a plan whereby the Closely Graded may be used as a Group Graded Series.

The Young People's Societies at the invitation of the United Society of Christian Endeavor formed a Topics Committee to prepare subjects and outlines for the young people's devotional meeting. These topics are now used by B. Y. P. U. A., Epworth League, Christian Endeavor, and other young people's organizations.

The Missionary Societies issue interdenominational mission-study courses annually on a foreign-mission theme and on a home-mission theme. These courses are graded for adults, young people, and juniors.

The Y. M. C. A. issues a program and material for their Pioneer and Comrade groups. The Y. W. C. A. does the same for the Girl Reserves. The Boy Scouts, Camp Fire Girls, and similar organizations issue program materials for their local units. Some organized class movements for young men and young women also issue material designed for use in a curriculum. Up to the present there is no understanding between these curriculum-making bodies looking toward some working agreement, although this varied material is expected to be used by groups in the same church. In addition to these regular sources of instructional and expressional material, several denominations through one or another board, or through a religious newspaper circulate special courses or study topics on such matters as stewardship, evangelism, church efficiency, vocational guidance, missionary reading courses, etc. This situation is largely responsible for the chaotic condition of the church curriculum.

## The Need of the Church

The first need of the church in this tangled curriculum situation is a competent leadership. We must develop a committee or Board of religious education who will have not only the name of the authority of the church behind them but a professional competence. They will need to distinguish sharply between organization and program. Most of the groups in the church engaged in religious education have been moulded into an organization whose form and name have been supplied from without, usually by a general organization of that name. This general organiza-

tion issues program material over the authority of its
name. Two problems are presented to local church leadership: The problem of organization—Is this the best form
of organization for our church?—and the problem of
curriculum—Is the program material the best possible for
that age group in our church?

A competent church committee on religious education
will make a patient study of the curriculum materials now
in use by the various groups of the church. It should
make this study sympathetically as it seeks to get the point
of view and purpose of the editor who has specialized in
the preparation of material and is seeking to serve many
similar groups in many dissimilar churches. The editor is
expecting his work to be adapted to local conditions by a
competent church leadership.

The church committee, from its independent study of
the general problem, should formulate a working theory
of the church curriculum. It will not anticipate a final
statement in view of the acknowledged perplexities of
professional educators. But the church is asking that a
beginning be made in defining the aim of the curriculum.
Probably the working theory as framed by the committee
will be modified many times in practise, but it will serve
its purpose if it is helping the church toward better things.

## Some Guiding Principles

We have behind us many years of experimenting with
various curriculum materials issued for church use. We
have ahead of us many years of further experimenting.
The best we can do now is to state some general principles
which have won a measure of agreement, and which will
give guidance to the church Board of Education.

### *1. The Curriculum Should Be Pupil-centered*

It should be written for the pupil more than the teacher. It should aim to enlist and direct the activity of the pupil.

### *2. The Curriculum Should Seek to Develop Personality in Its Fulness*

It will not be content with a ministry to one side of life but will seek to enrich the physical, intellectual, social, and religious.

### *3. The Curriculum Should Be Unified*

Instead of several curricula providing instruction and expression, unrelated and sometimes in disagreement, one general plan should operate for the whole church. This general plan will use various materials supplied from various sources, but it will move with a single purpose.

### *4. The Curriculum Should Be Biblical*

It must make central the great text-book of the church.

### *5. The Curriculum Should Be Comprehensive*

It will include all the subjects where instruction is needed. It will aim to train the various skills needed in the service of the church and the Kingdom. It will provide material necessary to special groups and organizations.

### *6. The Curriculum Should Be Evangelistic*

In all contacts with childhood and youth especially first place must be given to the purpose to make Jesus known as Friend and Saviour.

### 7. *The Curriculum Should Build the Church of Tomorrow*

The instruction should be consistent with the deep convictions of the church and call forth into service the workers and the leaders.

### 8. *The Curriculum Should Be Missionary*

It should carry the missionary message and appeal to all ages and all groups and be freighted with a deep concern for the evangelization of the whole world.

### 9. *The Curriculum Should Be Social*

It must seek the development of the individual, but it must not neglect the obligations of the church to the community and to society.

### 10. *The Curriculum Must Be Flexible*

Let us beware of making an educational scheme mechanical. Exalt the teacher and leader-friend over material and methods.

## Help for the Teacher

To discuss intelligently it is necessary first to define the terms we use so that this chapter seeks to define curriculum, then to understand its origin and the changing theories which have influenced its character to the present-day confused condition in the educational world and the corresponding difficulty concerning religious education. The need of the church is for a competent leadership, which may be a church committee to guide the church in shaping its curriculum. There are ten guiding principles enumerated which should influence such a committee in its work.

## Topics for Further Study

Test the curriculum of religious education in your local church by these guiding principles and tabulate the result.

Build a curriculum for the Junior child that will meet these tests around a project of providing a Christmas celebration for a family of foreigners living in the neighborhood.

## VI

## TRAINING IN WORSHIP

We have said that our first aim in religious education is to lead the child to an acquaintance with God. To know about God, his revelation, his works, his salvation, his commands, is not to know him. Information and theory can never take the place of the knowledge which can come only through that inner spiritual communion which we call prayer. As we thus come to know God through the revealing Christ, the Holy Spirit, the Bible, through all his creation, through communion, we are impelled to worship him. The Standard Dictionary defines worship as the feeling or the act of religious homage toward the Supreme God, an act or acts collectively of such homage, as at a given time and place, such as adoration, thanksgiving, prayer, praise, and offerings.

"In church, cottage, college, camp, on sea or land, around the world, wherever is adoring affection and trust toward him on high, expressed by the aspiring spirit, there is true worship."

### The Impulse to Worship Is Natural

It would seem that man by his very nature is impelled to worship, and it is not surprising to find acts of worship at the very core of all the great world religions. Doctor Zwemer tells in "Moslem Women" of a cultured, dark-skinned man who boarded a train in England. The narrator's companions said, "Hello, here comes a nigger."

81

Ignoring the implied sneer, the newcomer began a series of questions. Did they know the Mohammedan believed in prayer? Did they know when the prayer season came the Mohammedan would brook no interference, he *would* pray? How was it that in the diner he had not seen any Christians pause for grace?

The writer once watched two women crouching before a hideous idol in a Taoist temple in China and offering paper money to their god, and at another time and place saw a poor Japanese sister supplicating Buddha by alternately ringing a bell and clapping her hands.

Spencer, in " The Education of the Pueblo Child," says:

The education of the Pueblo which most nearly corresponds to that given by the schools in civilized countries is their religious education. This reaches into the minutest details of their lives which are one incessant round of formalistic observances. The acquiring of their elaborate ritual, which must be exactly transmitted and exactly used in order to be efficacious, is an educational task of no small proportions.

From India we have this:

Whatever oblation is offered, whatever is given when penance is performed, and whatever is done without faith, that, O Son of Pritha, is called Asat, and that is naught, both after death and here.

Jesus said, " God is a spirit, and they that worship him must worship him in spirit and in truth." Not only *whom* we worship but *how* becomes of first importance in religious education. Just as the Pueblo Indian understood that his religious ideas and ideals must be communicated and perpetuated in worship, so we realize that the vitalizing of the truth in the life can only come through that inner communion which constitutes true worship.

## We Need to Teach How to Worship

Is worship so spontaneous, so natural, so usual that there is no need to teach how to worship? If we teach about God, will all who hear know how to worship him? To some extent, yes. Yet the disciples watching Jesus closely, eager to emulate him, longing for his grace and power, were constrained to say, " Teach us to pray." As Jesus practised it, prayer is worship. Taking the disciples' prayer as taught them by Jesus for our worship model we find these six elements present in true worship: Praise and thanksgiving, confession of shortcoming, petition, consecration, and communion. The disciples understood that Jesus' sure hold upon God as Father and close Friend came from his close association with God as he worshiped him. To bring each individual into personal contact with God through Christ is the aim to be sought in all our worship. We are defining worship as a definite act or set of acts which consciously concern God and ourselves. The poet sang with truth, *Laborare est orare*—" To labor is to pray." The apostle said, " I show my faith by my works." Yet neither would deny the soul's need of definite approach to God in worship. How sadly true it is that many Christians even have never learned how to worship.

## What Are the Agencies Which Consciously or Unconsciously Are Teaching Us to Worship?

### *1. The Home*

The home may create an atmosphere of worship. There is no greater test of true religion than this. If the parents have a genuine love for Christ and a real reverence toward

God, in some sympathetic way the little child imbibes that same attitude; but if the pose is hypocritical and the words hollow, no formalism can supply the lack. In the home should be taught the earliest forms of prayer. Family worship in grace at meals, hymns at eventide, bedside prayers, and some regular occasion when the family meet together for prayer and praise preserve the spirit of worship.

## 2. The Church Service

What is the heritage in terms of worship which the church has passed on to her children? There is first of all the power of example. Here are gathered the leaders in the community, the adults of the home; " with one accord and in one place " they acknowledge God. There is, secondly, the atmosphere of worship which the church supplies. A certain great writer says that, though not a church-member, he continues to attend church because the combination of architecture, lights, shadows, and organ music creates a quiet of soul in which atmosphere he feels he can approach God. The hymns of the church express for the worshiper the desires of his heart in adoration, thanksgiving, supplication, and consecration. The Scripture reading and liturgical responses lead him further into an understanding of God's ways, and the public prayer seeks to voice the collective desire of the people's hearts. This service is usually planned for adults yet has made a definite contribution to the child's ideas of worship. The power of example, the message of the great hymns of the church, the repetition of Bible passages, even though not fully understood at the time, remain associated in the child's mind with the solemn hush and reverent attitude of all concerned, and contribute a sense of awe and majesty which he needs and which he is not likely to get in any other way.

### 3. Group Gatherings

The Church Prayer-meeting. This is a service designed, to judge by its name, expressly for the practise of worship. If the meeting fails to hold the church-members, it is a fair question to ask whether the cause is to be found in the lack of spirituality of the people, or the lack of worshipfulness of the service, or something of both conditions.

The Young People's Meeting. In the weekly young people's meeting there is a great opportunity to learn and practise true worship. All that is said, later, concerning the planning of the worship program of the Sunday school may be said of the devotional period in the young people's meeting.

Adult Church Societies, such as organized classes and women's circles. These offer an opportunity for training in the devotional life that the church should not neglect. Too often the worship period of the meeting consists of a poorly read passage, an unrelated hymn or solo, and a formal lip-prayer, when we need to worship or we die spiritually.

Various organizations for the children—Scouts, Mission Bands, Knights, etc. These present a field for instruction in true worship. The leader must be himself a worshiper in spirit and in truth, he must understand the child's need for variety, concreteness, directness, spontaneity, unconventionality. The worship period for a small group of children requires more preparation on the part of the leader than for a larger group. The attitude of reverence is less easily maintained. It requires knowledge of the age-characteristics of the group to know when and how to call out individual prayer.

## 4. *Private Devotions*

The church has sought at various times to help the individual worshiper by providing devotional books, prayer lists, prayer pledges, etc. From a Chinese hut came a confused murmur of voices. Peering through the open doorway the visitor saw a group of old women seated about a long table and industriously fingering their beads while they repeated the magic formula *Amidha-Va*. Even the Lord's Prayer may become a meaningless form of words thoughtlessly repeated. " The Book of Remembrance " compiled by the Baptist Board of Missionary Cooperation and similar prayer calendars published by other denominational missionary Boards are a direct contribution to the training of the devotional life of those who use them.

## 5. *The Sunday School*

The worship period of the Sunday school has long gone under the name of " opening exercises," and as " opening exercises " has seemed to serve almost any purpose other than that of true worship. A Sunday-school leadership which is rapidly passing did not seem to understand the significance of the opening period.

It has served, for instance:

To Create a Happy Atmosphere. Brightness and good cheer belong to child life and to the Christian life. They make attractive the Sunday school, therefore it is a legitimate purpose to seek to create such an atmosphere at the opening of the school session.

To Weld the Company Together. Joining together in song, led in united prayer, individuals of very diverse ages come to feel a common bond. The community sing movement which swept over England in 1927 is a case in point. On a great football field 100,000 persons, king and commoners, joined in singing " Abide With Me " and many popular airs.

To Rouse Enthusiasm. Older persons can remember the enthusiasm created by the first Moody and Sankey hymns. How lustily we sang them! Urged on by a leader who clapped his hands or beat time with his foot we often mistook noise for music, but we were enthusiastic.

To Fill a Gap. Something must be done while the tardy were gathering or to fill the interim between church and Sunday school, hence " opening exercises."

To Make a Place for a 'Sermonette. Many times it has seemed as if the whole thought of the leader was on the little talk upon the lesson he planned to give, the devotional period being merely incidental.

To Give Opportunity for the Presentation of Special Pleas, temperance, missionary, etc. These may be made a very vital part of worship, as we shall see, but are not the whole of it.

To Show Courtesy to Visiting Celebrities.

Some of these aims are legitimate and belong in a worship period, but none of them is adequate to lead to an understanding of true worship. However, these same " opening exercises " in the hands of devoted leaders have taught many thousands almost all they know of worship. They have supplied the note of praise and of social recognition of God. Can the church do better at the task of teaching her people to worship and how?

G

## What Are the Means We Use to Aid Us in Our Worship?

### *1. Physical Surroundings*

Writing home after visiting one of the great cathedrals of the old world, a young man said, " As I entered the door I appreciated for the first time the meaning of the line, ' A dim religious light,' but I welcomed with joy the clean shaft of sunlight streaming in through an open window and piercing the gloom with God's clear light of truth." Not dimness or mustiness, but harmony of line and color, that the senses may be at rest and the mind freed from earthly distractions, is what we need. Just as the beauty of a sunset lifts our hearts to the God of nature, so simplicity of line, harmony in coloring, neatness and orderliness in arrangement are essential to a proper environment for worship. Seats that are comfortable, so placed that all may hear and see, also help. No one would tolerate a tardy janitor who distributed books and arranged cushions after the church service had begun. Neither should an usher be allowed to seat people during prayer or Scripture reading. It is quite as important that all the machinery of conducting a Sunday school or other group gathering be attended to before the meeting begins. Suitableness and comfort of arrangements, orderliness in details, and order in participants are first helps in worship.

### *2. A Worship Plan*

(1) For the Church Service.

In the church service the sermon, choir selections, hymns, Scripture reading, and prayer center about one theme, supplementing or complementing each other, thus deepening and clarifying the impression they make upon the worshiper. If the choir music is selected without reference to the preacher's plans it is likely their effort will become a performance, not a worship. Almost equally disastrous is last-minute selection of Scripture and hymns. In a prescribed ritual some one else has done the planning; room for spontaneity and choice is no excuse for carelessness in planning.

The church ministers to an ungraded group. There are (or should be) old and young, simple and learned. How shall the worship period provide for them all? Various plans are being tried and the whole matter is still in the experimental stage. One plan is to form a Junior Church, giving the younger children a service of their own paralleling the adult service. This has the advantage of appealing to the children and making possible a complete worship period suited to their needs. Its disadvantage is the separation of families, the loss of dignity and awesomeness of the service, and the danger that the junior service deteriorate into a mere parody of the senior. Other plans have been tried, such as forming the children into Junior Choirs and giving them definite place on the church program, or dismissing the children to another room before the preaching of the sermon. Few pastors who try either of these two plans seem to remember the presence of the children in their public prayer or Scripture selection.

(2) For Various Groups.

The young people's societies and junior church groups have from the first emphasized the devotional period of their meetings, and the general and denominational organizations offer carefully planned programs for worship periods together with many suggestive helps for making the programs appealing and worth while. The necessity remains that the leader make prayerful preparation in order that the service may be in spirit (not mechanical) and in truth (not artificial or lip-service only).

Some of the groups within the church look to non-church organizations for their activities, as the Boy Scouts, for instance. The leaders are often chosen for some other reason than their skill in spiritual leadership. The worship period of these organizations becomes peculiarly the concern of the church or Sunday school. Who is planning for them and how?

(3) For the Sunday School.

One plea that Sunday-school superintendents used to make for the ungraded school and the uniform lesson was the comparative ease in arranging the worship period. It is quite true that graded worship requires a little more preparation. It is also true that it is many times more effective. Again, what is our aim? If it is to usher the pupils into the presence of God, to teach them how to come to him as Friend and Saviour, then how marvelously a little trouble will be repaid!

*a.* The first necessity is to have a plan, not for one session alone, but for a series of sessions, such as a year. In a loose-leaf note-book consider the worship themes for the year, giving to each a quarter.

For instance: Fall—Thanksgiving; Winter—Giving; Spring—Dedication; Summer—God, the Father.

Then split the Thanksgiving topic into: October—Rejoicing as His Children, Rallying to His Service; November—Grateful for His Provision; December—Thankful for Jesus, the Christ.

Having chosen a theme, select Scripture passages, hymns, stories, pictures, dramatic presentations to fit the theme. Decide on a hymn that may be repeated each Sunday until it can be sung without the hymn-book, also choose some verse or passage that the school will learn during the month or quarter.

*b.* The next step is to plan for each service.

It will be necessary to decide upon the exact amount of time for the worship period, varying from ten minutes with the little children to twenty-five for the adults. At what time in the session shall the worship period be held? At the beginning? This plan is followed by the majority of schools. Or at the close? Most authorities think the ideal plan is for the teacher to close the class with a class prayer. With the littlest people the worship period may come at any point in the program where it is appropriate.

*c.* In planning worship programs introduce variety. This is very important with the junior grades, but helps to hold the interest with all. Sometimes open with prayer, sometimes with an instrumental piece, and close with a story or a hymn.

*d.* We must take account of special days. The tendency today is for the ardent advocate of any cause to ask the church for a Sunday. Indeed, most of them do not ask but announce and expect the churches to fall in line. Should any church seriously attempt to set aside a Sunday for each of the special causes thus soliciting her help, would there be Sundays enough in the year? The leader must determine what special days to observe in the Sunday school and plan his program accordingly, jealously guarding the worship period from unnecessary intrusion.

*e.* The choice of the Scripture passage. This may be read in concert from the Bible or responsively from a specially prepared order of service. It may be recited from memory or be read by the leader or by a selected class. It may be illustrated by picture or by a dramatic presentation. If a church owns a stereopticon it is possible by the use of architects' tracing paper over the lens to show the pictures by daylight. Denominational missionary boards now have beautiful pictures together with explanatory lectures which they loan to churches. A dramatic presentation of a Bible story or a missionary message, if thoughtfully given by those who have carefully rehearsed, makes a deep impression. But the "if" is significant. The actors must realize the importance of their part and must not be slipshod or bungling.

*f.* The selection of the hymns. Surely if a superintendent once realized that he was selecting songs for no less a purpose than to lead the pupils into the presence of God, he would not be tempted by unworthy music or cheap sentiment because of its catchiness or seeming brightness. The public school has proved that children enjoy good music and sing it heartily and happily. The leader who mistakes shouting for singing encourages lawlessness and disrespect without gaining the brightness and enthusiasm he is really seeking. The program-maker should consult with the music-leader. The hymns should be as carefully planned as any other part of the worship service. The choice should include at least one of the tried hymns of the church and be repeated often enough to become a permanent possession of the pupils.

Miss Main in her book, "Religious Education Music Manual," says: "A hymn must embody rhythm, expression, devotion. A song must embody rhythm, expression, and an idea worth while."

In choosing hymns for children to sing she gives the following suggestions:

> The song must be understandable.
>
> Before singing tell a story which will illustrate the song. Repeat the words of the entire hymn, and have the children tell you what it is about.
>
> Have the pianist play it over twice.
>
> Repeat verse by verse, having the child give it back to you in substance.
>
> Have the pianist play over the melody. Have the children hum the second time it is played.
>
> Let the teacher sing the entire hymn through at least twice.
>
> Let the teacher sing the first verse, having the children sing it after her.
>
> Repeat until all the verses have been sung.

A leader is much helped in making up his program if he has a good hymn-book. The tendency of many leaders is to use only a few of the hymns in a book and entirely neglect many others, with the result that the school tires of the repetition long before the book is exhausted. Simple melody, rich but not complicated harmony, both suited to the thought expressed, are characteristics of good hymns. The time may be vigorous and with a well-marked beat but should not suggest the ragtime of the streets.

### 3. The Offering as a Part of Worship

The worship period is lacking indeed that does not include a place for the dedication of oneself and one's means.

We give as a matter of conviction and duty, but we give as an act of worship. The preacher who announces, " The collection will now be taken," has missed for himself and his people the true meaning of the offering. The prayer before the offering is received or the prayer or congregational response afterward places the offering in its true place as a part of the worship service. This applies to all of the groups equally well. An essential part of worship is consecration of ourselves and of our means. But if the money is gathered with no consecrating word of prayer or verse of Scripture it becomes a collection of dues or taxes. In the Sunday-school worship program there should be a time and place for the offering. If individual envelopes are used ushers may pass the plates, and each one may drop in his envelopes as in the church service. If the offering is taken by classes, this should be done first, and then the ushers collect the class envelopes. In either case, there should be a consecrating verse or hymn. When this nation was younger and poorer we had in the church Female Mite Societies to which women pledged one cent a week, and there grew up in our Primary Department a devotion to the little song " Hear the Pennies Dropping." This may have been all right years ago, but just as the missionary mite idea has expanded to the thought of a stewardship of all we have as from the Lord, so our thought concerning the children is that they shall learn to give as they are able. The Lord's work needs more than the pennies. We must not limit the children's thought to our smallest coin. A very impressive service may be had in the Sunday school by having the class representatives come with their gifts to the desk for the consecrating prayer.

## 4. We Need to Grade Our Worship Plans

It is evident from the matters we have already discussed in this chapter that we need to grade our worship program to suit the understanding and age-characteristics of the different groups with which we deal. In the church service the child will get something from the usual adult worship program, but he will get much more if some portion of that program is planned especially for him. A while ago some four hundred ministers gathered in New York City to discuss the absence of children from the regular church service and as a result of their discussion announced a city-wide " Bring Your Child to Church Sunday." A keen critic of the preachers said their conclusions were beside the mark. The real question was, " Is there anything in our service that will appeal to the child? "

If the Sunday school must meet in one room so that it is impossible to separate for the worship period, the leader should plan his program with the junior, intermediate, and young people's groups in mind, especially.

### MODEL PROGRAMS

The following model programs for different age groups are based upon suggestions given by experts in each of these special fields.

#### PRIMARY

In the *Children's Leader,* for the Primary Department, Margaret M. Clemens, taking for the month the theme " Thoughts of the Heavenly Father," and for the first Sunday, " Our Father's Love," plans this program:

WORSHIP PERIOD.

*Prelude.* Andante. (From Sonata in C Major. Beethoven.)

CALL TO WORSHIP.

*Superintendent.* This is the day which the Lord hath made.

*Pupils.* We will rejoice and be glad in it.

*All* (sing). "Sunday, Happy Sunday."

*Superintendent.* Every morning seems to say,

> There's something happy on the way,
> And God sends love to you.

I can think of many ways in which God sent love to me this morning. The good breakfast I had and the bright sunshine out-of-doors tell me of the heavenly Father's love. Can you think of some way by which God sends love to you? (Let the children suggest.)

POEM. "He Doth Love Us."

SONG. "Praise Him, Praise Him." ("Songs for Little People.")

PRAYER. (Thanking the heavenly Father for his love as it is shown in the things mentioned by the children.)

RECITATION of Memory Verses about God's love. (Taken from beginners and primary, first and second year Graded Lessons.)

SONG. "He'll Not Forget His Little Ones." ("First Book in Hymns and Worship.")

OFFERING SERVICE.

*Superintendent.* Our Father in heaven shows his love for us by giving us so many things. I am glad we can bring gifts to him too. Let us give our love gifts now.

(Pianist plays while offering is being taken.)

*Offering Song.*

> Since my heavenly Father
> Gives me everything,
> Lovingly and gladly
> Now my gift I bring.

CLOSING HYMN.  "Saviour, Again to Thy Dear Name We Raise."

PRAYER.

DISMISSAL.

### INTERMEDIATE

Taking "God Our Father" as the theme for the month and "Our Father's Love" as the theme for the first Sunday, Dr. J. Sherman Wallace in the *Young People's Leader* has prepared the following worship program for Intermediates:

INSTRUMENTAL MUSIC.  (Bright and joyful but not boisterous.)

CALL TO WORSHIP (by leader).  Our worship theme for this month is "God Our Father." The theme of our worship today is "Our Father's Love." Let us express our appreciation of his love by singing, "This Is My Father's World."

WORSHIP IN SONG.  "This Is My Father's World." (First and second stanzas.  Sung by all.)

CALL TO CHRISTIAN LIVING.  Be sons of your Father who is in heaven (Matt. 5: 45).  (First repeated by leader, then repeated by all.)

SONG.  Third stanza, "This Is My Father's World."

WORSHIP WITH SCRIPTURE.  Matthew 5: 1-16.  (Read antiphonally; men and boys reading first verse, women and girls reading second verse, etc.)

TALK (by a man teacher).  Our God is a God of love, in contrast with heathen gods in ancient times and in modern times.  (Two minutes.)

PRAYER (by a man teacher).  Thanking God for his love for us, for the world he has given us, for his provision for our lives, for the gift of his Son, Jesus.  Ask that we may appreciate his love and be at all times worthy of it.  (In terms of intermediates.  Two minutes.)

SONG.  "There's a Wideness in God's Mercy."

OFFERINGS.  (Make offerings by classes.  Let a boy and a girl bring offerings to the front.  While they still hold the offerings, all stand and sing the first stanza of "I'll Live for Him." While all are standing, the leader offers short prayer of consecration of gifts, as "Lord, take our gifts as an expression of our love for thee.")

BENEDICTION (by all). Our heavenly Father, may thy love be around us like the sunshine that warms us, like the air that invigorates us, and like a wall that protects us. Thou art our Father, may we be thy true children. (Memorize or read from blackboard.)

## YOUNG PEOPLE

With "The Church" for the month's theme and "The Church's Influence" as the theme for the fourth Sunday, Charles A. Boyd, also in the *Young People's Leader,* gives this suggestive program:

INSTRUMENTAL PRELUDE. Hymn, "O Zion, Haste, Thy Mission High Fulfilling."

CALL TO WORSHIP. (Isa. 55:11.)

PRAYER (by a class president or group leader). (It is suggested that the prayer be especially one of thankfulness for the influence of the church in all lands and in many phases of life.)

HYMN. The chosen hymn for October—"The Church's One Foundation" (verses two and three).

SPECIAL FEATURE. "The Church's Influence in Present-day Life." (A five- or eight-minute talk by some prominent business or professional man of the community.)

SOLO. "From Age to Age They Gather." (The assembly might join in the chorus.)

READING. An old hymn of the church.

OUR OFFERING for the Extension of the Church's Influence.

DEDICATORY PRAYER. (By the leader.)

BENEDICTION. "The Lord bless thee and keep thee, the Lord make his face to shine upon thee, and be gracious unto thee."

## ADULTS

In the *International Journal of Religious Education* Frances Willard Woodall, using the theme "Christian Growth in the New Year," has for the second Sunday "Christian Growth Through

Prayer," with the following suggested program[1] for an adult department:

PRELUDE. "Sweet Hour of Prayer."

PRAYER. The Lord's Prayer.

HYMN. "The Earth Is Hushed in Silence."

POEM. "One Short Hour" (read in unison).

> Lord, what a change within us one short hour
>    Spent in thy presence will prevail to make
>    What heavy burdens from our bosoms take,
> What parched grounds refresh as with a shower!
> We kneel, and all around us seems to lower;
>    We rise, and all, the distant and the near,
>    Stand forth in sunny outline brave and clear;
> We kneel, how weak; we rise, how full of power!
>    Why, therefore, should we do ourselves this wrong,
>    Or others, that we are not always strong,
> That we are overborne with care,
>    That we should ever weak or heartless be,
> Anxious or troubled, when with us is prayer,
>    And joy and strength and courage are with thee?
>
> *—Archbishop Trench.*

SOLO. "Lord, for Tomorrow and Its Needs."

SCRIPTURE. Psalm 44: 1-4a, 20, 21; 19: 12-14.

HYMN. "Rock of Ages, Cleft for Me."

SCRIPTURE. John 17, "The Prayer of Jesus."

HYMN. "Nearer, My God, to Thee."

POEM. "My Task."

WORSHIP THROUGH OFFERING.

PRAYER. (By leader.)

RESPONSE (sung softly). "Take My Life and Let It Be."

POEM. "Three Doors."

HYMN. "Sweet Hour of Prayer."

SILENT PRAYER.

BENEDICTION.

[1] Reproduced here by permission of The International Council of Religious Education, owner of copyright.

As before noted if the school meets for its worship period as one body it will be found best to base the programs upon an Intermediate or young people's model, or even occasionally with the Juniors more particularly in mind.

## Help for the Teacher

This chapter seeks to show that: (1) While a man has a natural impulse to worship a Being higher than himself, as shown in examples from other religions, and (2) since through prayer in worship all that he learns of God becomes vital in his life, he needs (a) to learn how to worship from Jesus' teaching and example, and (b) he needs helps to worship from his home and his church. (3) Man is aided in worship by suitable physical surroundings, by a plan of service, which includes the music, Scripture reading, prayer, talk, and offering. (4) Our worship service should be graded, or if it must serve an ungraded group, it should recognize the different ages in its program.

## Questions for Further Study

1. Make a study of the worship periods in your church service, church school, and other organizations. Suggest changes for making them more helpful.

2. Define for yourself what is meant by worship.

3. What is the value of family worship?

4. How can it be maintained today?

5. What is the function of public prayer?

# TRAINING IN SOCIAL LIVING

## Two Problems Confronting the Church

The church of today finds itself confronted with two problems which at first seem wide apart but upon closer inspection are found to have much in common. On the one hand, there is a world of human beings who after nearly two thousand years of Jesus' teaching that love is the supreme law of life, still depend upon force to settle their differences and build their economic structure upon competition. Though millions call themselves by the name of Him who taught, " One is your father, and all ye are brethren," they yet draw sharp racial lines and treat seemingly less-favored peoples as though inferiors in the sight of God. This is a day when as never before a non-Christian world is challenging the church to live as she professes.

The standards set up by Jesus do not differ from what they always have been, but our understanding of the implications of his command, " Follow me," is clearer. " I have many more things to say to you, but you cannot bear them now," he told his disciples, and as we have followed him afar off, we have begun to discern what some of these things may be. How shall the church persuade a selfish, unseeing people to walk in the Jesus road of absolute love and service?

The other problem is the desire for recreation and social life which is natural to all children and adults. In

H                                                                    103 spite of the frowns and prohibitions of the church, the children of the church have continued to play, the youth have had their pastimes, and adults their recreations. Has the one problem any bearing upon the other, and what should the church do concerning them?

## Man Is a Social Being

We have come to understand today that man is a social being in the sense that no human being can live unto himself alone. When a tiny baby comes into the home his very life is dependent upon doctor, nurse, mother, and father. And his coming directly affects them. For the parents, indeed, his coming means an entire rearrangement of their manner of life and their plans for the future. And as individuals interact upon each other, so does family upon family, so do groups upon other groups, states and nations upon each other. When I was the only child in the family it was right for me to eat both pieces of candy from the plate, but when my little brother came I had to learn to share. Once the people of the United States thought of themselves as a separated people. Now they are beginning to realize that what other nations do hurts or helps them, and vice versa, our action affects all other peoples. The health, the moral standards, the economic status, the political actions, the religious ideals of one have their influence upon all.

Our whole theory of education is affected by this fact of our social interrelation. Our aim in education becomes an effort to prepare the individual to take his rightful place among his fellows, and our method of educating him includes the influence of his fellows upon him. Educating is a socializing process.

*An appreciation of this fact that man is a social being affects our ideas of religious education.* Jesus taught, "What shall it profit a man if he gain the whole world and lose his own soul," and in the early centuries of the Christian era men came to put the major emphasis upon the saving of the individual soul for its own sake, through a failure to appreciate the relation of this teaching to his whole body of teaching. Just as emphatically Jesus said, "Seek ye first the kingdom of God."

A kingdom cannot be an individual, it must be a social institution. The Master who cried so passionately, "Whoso causeth one of these little ones to suffer, it were better for him that a millstone were hanged about his neck, and that he were drowned in the midst of the sea," was thinking also of the good of all as well as of the opportunity for individual growth in grace when he commanded, "He that would be great among you, let him be the servant of all." It naturally follows then that the church, while seeking to lead the individual to a knowledge of and allegiance to Christ, must be concerned to make plain to him all the social implications of this allegiance.

*The church must train for social living.* This does not mean mass conversion as practised by the early Jesuit fathers who in their zeal are said to have sprinkled the holy water over whole villages and then moved on to further conquests. Society is made up of individuals who must individually be won to Christ, but having come to him they need to learn the Jesus way of living together. "Thou shalt love the Lord thy God, and thy neighbor as thyself."

Jesus' world, in other words, is the world of persons in relations with each other. For him all the supreme and primary values of

Play is not trivial; it is highly serious and of deep significance. To the calm keen vision of one who truly knows human nature, the spontaneous play of the child discloses the future inner life of the man.

Aside from the value of play in strengthening the body and preparing the child through imitation for adult activities, we have discovered that through play the child learns certain character lessons of great social and spiritual significance. In organized games he learns to submit to rules, to obey a leader, to sacrifice his own advantage for the sake of the team; he learns loyalty to his comrades, to honor impartiality and give justice. He learns self-control and democratic principles of self-government. He learns to respect the property rights of others, to honor the truth and hate a lie. He gains power of initiative and leadership. He learns to value others for qualities other than accidents of birth which may have made them rich or poor. These lessons are fundamental character lessons and as such are of vital concern to the church.

## The Church and the Children's Play Problem

It is unhappily true that many children never have any play life at all. Because of the poverty of their parents and the greed of employers there are little children of six and seven and even younger who work in mills or in the fields eight, nine, and ten hours a day. Stunted in body, dulled of mind, starved of spirit these little ones cry out to the Christian church to cease not to preach and to labor for their emancipation. Many more of the world's children play amid surroundings and under circumstances that teach them the exact opposites of the qualities we have mentioned. For courtesy and consideration they learn roughness and cruelty; their lessons in leadership are lessons in craftiness and force; their imagination is exercised not upon the natural and the beautiful, but upon the vile and evilly suggestive; their gang loyalty spells other-gang hatred. Once Christian people understand that through play the child can be led to practise the Christlike qualities or have fastened upon him habits that lead him away from Christ, they must see the necessity of providing for the children of the church opportunities for play in such surroundings and under such leadership as shall ensure the best results for health and character.

1. The church can help parents to understand the importance of play in the life of the child. It can furnish parents with books suggesting suitable games for children. Too many parents look upon the playtime as an opportunity to be free from responsibility; far too few know how to play with their children. We are concerned over the weakening of home ties today. The home that provides the children with simple games in which all the family take an interest, where quarreling is not allowed but skill in competition is encouraged; the home that always has a welcome for the children's friends and teaches them to play by playing with them, will probably never need to complain of the children's drifting in the years to come.

2. Even if the community provides a playground for the children, the church needs a place where the children of the church may play under proper leadership, both because of the training in character that comes through play and because the teacher who plays with the children understands them better and has better opportunity to become their friend and leader. The play program for the chil-

dren of the church should include play periods for different age groups, special programs for church and national holidays, party occasions when friends and parents are entertained, competitive games and exercises for the intermediate boys and girls. Plans for summer outings with camping for the boys and girls should be part of this program. Such a recreational program requires supervision and leadership. There are helpful books on graded play for the guidance of volunteer workers. In all this one great concern of the church is that the play of its children shall be properly correlated with the whole church program of religious education. It is as easy for a church to drain its energies all into the recreational program as to go to the other extreme and exclude play from its program entirely.

3. The church has said to her children, " Thou shalt not " go here or there, do thus and so, but has not always seen the equal or greater necessity to say, " Come, do this better, safer, happier thing." Any church in a community, urban or rural, that has no playground for the children, can do certain definite things. It can rouse public sentiment as to the need for a playground, it can lead in organizing a playground association, it can urge its membership to give the movement financial support, it can insist that the playground have proper supervision.

## The Church and the Young People's Play Problem

The church has tried to control the exuberance of young life, the desire for play, and the longing for companionship by prohibitions and has never succeeded. Normal young people in the late teens and early twenties crave the society of other young people, they need and will find relaxation and a good time in play and sports and social intercourse. Yet through indifference, carelessness, and ignorance this natural craving for sociability leads many to give pleasure an undue proportion of their time; while others are led through evil associations far astray.

What can the church do to help her young people in this respect?

1. The church can maintain a sympathetic attitude. The most frequent complaint heard from young people is " No one understands." By circulating books in physiology and psychology, by inviting men and women who have been successful workers with young people to speak to them, the church may help the adult members, parents, officers, teachers to a sympathetic understanding of the young people.

2. The church that has laid a foundation of right relations toward its junior and intermediate boys and girls, has the advantage of a group of young people whose good times and social contacts have had the church for their center.

3. The church can provide a suitable place for social meetings. Home missionaries have not hesitated to hold services in schoolhouses or dance-halls if no church building was available, yet there are all over this country little church buildings which are the only clean and decent place for the social gathering of the people, that are tightly locked six days in the week while the forces of evil have their own way.

4. The church can encourage the young people to take the initiative and plan their own recreational program. A supervisor is needed with the younger groups; with the young people, a wise and tactful counselor.

5. The church can introduce the young people to new forms of amusement. Many Christian young people seem to acquire a sort of inferiority complex on their social side. They assume that, if they cannot conscientiously go with the crowd and do as the crowd does, then they must remain shut out from social life. Last winter a young woman in Philadelphia had a worth-while idea. She had been reading the letters from young people printed in an evening paper, and she argued how foolish for so many of us to spend our time bewailing the fact that we do not like petting parties, that we disapprove of wild parties, and imagine that therefore nobody loves us, and we might as well go out in the garden and eat woolly worms. The others call us slow; very well, we will call ourselves slow. She organized a " slow " club, others seized upon the idea, and in a few months slow clubs sprang up all over Philadelphia. Some of these clubs were literary societies, some were dramatic clubs, there were travel and study clubs, hiking parties; while some organized athletic teams of various sorts. They met in Christian and Hebrew Association buildings, in halls and churches and homes.

This movement demonstrated several things, among others these two: That once they get the idea young people are quite capable of initiating and regulating their own social life; and that there are many different kinds of social diversions open to young people. Any one who will take the trouble to question a class of young people will be surprised to find how many really know no other means of entertaining than dancing. To introduce them to this wealth of social possibilities is a worth-while service.

6. The church may train certain young people to be

leaders in organized play. Through organized play the awkwardness of those unaccustomed to social usages is overcome; unsuspected powers of leadership are developed, minds are stimulated, lives are brightened, and young people at the mating age are brought together under wholesome, happy conditions. Experience in conducting socials is a great help, but most leaders are the better for a course in organized play at some Summer Assembly or Winter Institute.

7. The church needs to correlate the social program with the remainder of the religious educational program. Are some groups giving undue emphasis to the social life? Do there seem to be some young people for whom no provision has been made?

8. The church may give the young people an opportunity to study the place and function of amusement in their own lives. They should be led to formulate standards of conduct for their social gatherings.

9. The church can help the young people to overcome the tendency to clannishness and snobbery by encouraging frequent general gatherings and by tactfully bringing forward now one group, now another.

10. As with the children, so with the young people, the church must be concerned that there is opportunity for wholesome social life amid morally and physically safe surroundings. Some church-members believe that the dance-hall is wholly evil, therefore if it cannot be suppressed it should be ignored. Others feel that since it exists it is the duty of the church to see that it is regulated. Certainly the church should lead in a community demand to provide for the young people places of meeting and programs of entertainment free from evil associations. Many young

people have the idea that the Christian life is one of repression and gloom. The church social program may be the means of disabusing their minds and of introducing them to the Master of the abundant life.

## The Adults and the Church

The pressure of years, the cares and responsibilities of life take from the adult the exuberance of youth, yet he finds a real need for play for the recreation of mind and body. Very many adults have forgotten how to play. They seem to have lost the power and the inclination to be sociable, yet all about them are other folks starving for the friendly word and kindly handclasp. The church needs to cultivate this social spirit in its members by making occasions for informal gatherings, by introducing simple get-together games, by presenting platform programs.

" This is a friendly church " is the sign over the door of a large city church that lives up to its slogan. It is probably true that the drawing and holding power of most successful adult Bible classes is that feeling of friendliness shown in all the meetings and fostered by the social gatherings of the class.

## The Present Recreational Problem

We have been discussing the church and the recreational problem quite as if there had been no change either in type of recreation offered or in people's attitude toward it in the last few years, but we are all aware that as a matter of fact there have been very great changes. As a people we have greater leisure for recreation. The shorter working-day gives to all classes more hours for recreation, and in many cases labor agitation brings this needed reform to our economic life ahead of any preparation by the church or the community to provide a place for the people to spend their leisure time or any organized community amusements.

The earliest community interest in play was shown in the Boston sand gardens for children. Gradually play facilities were provided for children of all ages, not only in the summertime but all the year around. At one time playgrounds depended upon churches or private individuals for support, but more and more communities are undertaking the support and control of them. With the playground has come the play teacher, for experience quickly demonstrated that undirected play sometimes turned over the playground to the bully, whereas directed play could teach the children many valuable character and citizenship lessons.

From the playground service to the children, communities have moved on to many forms of recreational service, community sings and choruses, folk dances and pageantry, band concerts, Fourth of July celebrations, the community Christmas tree, twilight baseball teams, etc. Where these wholesome community plans for the people's leisure do not exist, the church should lead in creating them; where they already exist, the church has a distinct duty in keeping their standard high.

The recreational problem has become complicated by the increased prosperity of our people. This allows us to go farther afield for our amusements. It has brought in the whole problem of young people, and the automobile, and youth spending money upon pleasure which he has not earned by his own labor and of whose value he has therefore no proportionate idea. It is responsible for the demand for more and more expensive forms of entertainment.

The recreational problem has undergone change in that whereas the people were once participators, they have become largely spectators. This development was almost inevitable as people became crowded in the cities where they were strangers to each other and separated by race and language. A people weary from the intensive drive of the modern business world easily learned to take its pleasure watching the professional sports player. There is a healthy reaction to this in the many local baseball clubs, public golf clubs, and tennis clubs that have sprung up of late years.

The recreational problem has become more acute because this added leisure and greater surplus have come to a people unprepared culturally to use and enjoy their opportunities. There is a Scotch proverb that the devil tempts all men, but idle men tempt the devil. What shall those who have never learned to love good reading, art, or music do with this precious recreation period? Classes, lectures, musical programs that open up to the people new sources of joy help solve this problem. A hobby, whether it be for collecting stamps or collecting newpaper jokes, may redeem leisure moments and brighten busy ones. Workers with boys discovered this some time ago. We need to give it wider application.

*The love for the drama is inherent in all of us.* The worship of primitive people is quite largely in dramatic form to gain attention to the message. Through pageantry communities are able to teach history and morals to the people. The church is discovering that through dramatic presentation hearts may be touched, interest aroused, information conveyed, and ideals be presented. The community that has been content to sit passively before the indifferent professional performer is having its dramatic taste elevated through active participation in community plays. The church that felt obliged to condemn the stage is learning the great educational and uplifting possibilities of the drama rightly used. The silent drama, the moving picture, has brought a new and pressing recreational problem. Here is an inexpensive means of recreation made available to millions of people. It is delightful, relaxing, amusing; it may be educative and uplifting. The church is presented with two immediate duties: the one is to use all its powers to persuade and compel the moving-picture industry to safeguard the moral character of its films; the other is to help its people to discriminate between the good and the bad film. A local theater is not indifferent to the demands of its clientele, and the church people can do much to influence the sort of film shown in their immediate neighborhood.

Within the limitations of this chapter it has been possible merely to suggest some of the ways in which the church may through its recreational program inculcate the graces of Christian character and remove temptation from the path of the young; in a word, make plainer to all the Jesus way of living together in sweetness and wholesomeness, sympathetically, understandingly, joyfully.

Henry A. Atkinson, in " The Church and the People's Play," says:

The prime task for the church is to help establish a standard for recreation for the community, and then help the community to find and maintain a proper balance between work and play.[1]

[1] From " The Church and the People's Play," by Henry A. Atkinson. Used by permission of The Pilgrim Press.

## Help for the Teacher

Since man cannot live unto himself alone, religious education must seek to train him to live among his fellows in the Christian way. Because of the child's natural impulse to play and the need of young and old for relaxation and recreation, through its recreational program the church may (1) train character, (2) remove temptation, (3) develop leaders, (4) improve community conditions, (5) become again the center of community life, (6) demonstrate the joyousness and fulness of the Christian life. The church has a particular service to each age group in the church and community. The present day presents special recreational problems to be solved.

## Questions for Further Study

A survey of the recreational needs of a local community with suggestions as to what the church should do about them.

A study of the recreational life of one age group in the church asking: Is it wholesome, helpful, under proper supervision, are all included, does it bind this group to the church? Make suggestions as to what is needed.

# VIII

## TRAINING THROUGH SERVICE

Love shows itself in service. Even a very casual study of Jesus' teaching should be enough to convince one that the great touchstone by which he judged every life was that of loving service. "Love the Lord thy God—and thy neighbor." "Inasmuch as ye did it unto the least of these, ye did it unto me." "Lovest thou me?" then, "Feed my lambs." And he "showed his love toward us in that, while we were yet sinners, he died for us." His terse command is, "Follow me." It would seem fair to say that his measure of every life is the measure of the service that life gives through love even to the extremity of laying down the life as he did. The exactions of his demand have not been changed by the years. In the measure we withhold loving service in that measure we follow him afar off.

### The Difficulties of the Application of This Principle in Our Day

The first difficulty is age-old. It confronted Esther when called upon to risk her life for the sake of her people; the rich young ruler faced it when he sought the way of salvation. We all want to be saved, and if church, ritual, or almsgiving could do it, how easy would be the way! To all our selfishness Jesus answers, "Go, sell all that thou hast, and come, follow me." Human nature

I

has not changed, and love of self is still the great obstacle to loving service.

But present-day conditions do seem to increase our difficulties somewhat. Once a Dorcas society could make garments for the poor neighbors and fulfil its obligation; today that little group of faithful women have expanded into Orphanages, Children's Aid Societies, Charity Bureaus, Welfare Federations. Loving service has reached out to include not alone the neighbors' children but the children of the world. The remoteness of much of the work dims our vision unless our sympathetic imagination has been cultivated. Another difficulty arises from the fact that the Christian ideal has so permeated Western civilization that the essential Christian character of many philanthropic enterprises has been lost sight of. Christians tend to limit their service to the standard of others, not gauge it by the standard of Jesus, who said, " Let your righteousness exceed that of the scribes and Pharisees."

The complexity of the problem of service tends to discourage the Christian whose impulse to serve is weak. Jesus started us on the way of service with the cup of cold water to the thirsty wayfarer. Through following his leadership we are confronted today with the problems which lie back of the wanderer's immediate thirst and hunger. What are the causes of unemployment? How can we insure justice to all? How prevent crime? How reform the criminal? Questions so complex, so far-reaching as to discourage the ordinary Christian and make him feel justified, not knowing what to do, in doing nothing.

Another great obstacle to loving service in the way of the modern Christian is the comparative prosperity the Christian in this country enjoys. When we are comfortable ourselves we easily forget the uncomfortable. How frequently one hears the remark: " I think I've done enough. It's some one's else turn now." A missionary returning after seven years of service in China was asked what most impressed him in his homecoming, and he replied: " The prosperity on every hand. Even our poorest do not know poverty as we see it in China." There is among us an easy philosophy that persuades our souls to take our ease, satisfied with a very little service. Yet the demand of Jesus is unchanged; he that saveth his life shall lose it. How shall the church train in service?

## Training in the Spirit of Service Should Begin in the Home

The most effective teaching is done by example. The parents who practise loving service toward each other and their neighbors make easy a similar attitude in the hearts of the children. But it is an all too common experience to find a home in which father or mother or both are self-sacrificing, even self-effacing, with an unwisdom that makes the children exacting and selfish. Parents need help in training their children for character building. In the Mothers' Class, the Home Department, the occasional sermon for parents, the church has an opportunity to show parents how they may inculcate this fundamental attitude of love and sacrifice, this serving habit of mind which must precede any missionary or social service. Mother does not want any of baby's cookie, but baby must learn to share, so she takes a real bite when it is offered to her. Sharing one's good times and one's privileges needs practical application all through family life. Consideration for the feelings of others, quiet when father is tired, pride when brother wins a prize, teaches sympathy. Sharing the family burdens is a lesson more easily learned in the family of the poor than that of the rich. Every child, rich or poor, should have some task which makes him a real contributor to the comfort of the home. He should give some service for that which he receives. It is of little character value for the child to carry to church and Sunday school the money father hands out. From earliest childhood the home needs to teach a true spirit of giving of that which costs us something. Thus sharing pleasures, burdens, sympathy, teaching to share through the actual doing, the home lays as a foundation the habit and attitude of service on which the Kingdom of God is built.

## Training in the Spirit of Service Should Continue in the Church

Years ago I knew a church which kept a book in which each new member on the day he was received into the church recorded the form of service he was ready to offer. But many do not know the needs of the church or realize their own possibilities in service. Doctor Kirtley suggests to the young Christian, See how much you can do, not how little, and do at some time more than you think you can. Children may help to beautify the church or may act as messengers for the pastor; boys and girls may be used in choirs or as ushers. In a ringing speech at the Northern Baptist Convention in Chicago the President of the B. Y. P. U. of A. plead with the church to give to mature young people tasks worthy of their ability, putting upon them real responsibility for church service, a house-to-house evangelistic effort, for instance. To have a church organized for education means a constant demand for teachers.

Here is a field of service which calls for consecration and training. To be a teacher is to occupy a place of special privilege. The church ought to exalt this service in the eyes of the young people and provide for their adequate preparation for its duties. The church is a company of volunteer workers most of whom need training, all of whom need exercising in church usefulness.

## Training in the Spirit of Service Must Reach Out Into All the World

Probably it could be said of the majority of Christian homes as of many who do not acknowledge Christ, that in them is to be found the spirit of loving service to one another. Indeed, if it were not so the whole fabric of our civilization, depending as it does upon the home, would collapse. Many Christians have responded to the demand upon them to give service to the local church, but the follower of Jesus cannot stop there, the Christian church cannot stop there, Jesus did not stop there. His is a message for all the world; he died that all might be saved, he commanded, " Go ye into all the world." The law of life for individual, for home, for church is the same; life lived unto itself is death, to save the life it must be lost.

" And preach the gospel to every creature." The obligation to pass on the good news rests upon every Christian without exception. Korean Christians are known for their missionary zeal because with them one of the qualifications for church-membership is the bringing of another to Christ. How shall the church train its membership in missionary service? Missionary training takes three forms: (1) Missionary education in the needs of the world, the history of missionary endeavor, the plans denominational and interdenominational for missionary extension, present-day missionary problems; (2) the immediate support of the missionary enterprises of the church by sacrificial prayer and giving; (3) actual practise in carrying out the command, each follower of Jesus himself a missionary.

## Missionary Education Should Be Graded

### *1. Primary*

In missionary as in all education we begin with the simple and the concrete. In the primary department the aim of missionary education is to make real to the child that the love of the heavenly Father includes all of his children everywhere. To do this there must be included in the educational program for these years stories of little folks of other lands, songs that include the world's children, a prayer that takes in the neighbors, gifts other than money of something the children have learned some other child really needs, gifts of money to the church missionary offering as part of their training in loyalty to the church program even though the ultimate use of the money is not fully understood by them; stories brought in by the children themselves of loving service to neighbor children. Service may take the form of gathering story papers to take to a sick child, bringing fruit or flowers for the same purpose, visits to a near-by needy family. Scrap-book pictures may be gathered, to be sent to home or foreign missionaries, always provided the children's own interest is aroused and stories help them to follow their gifts in imagination. Denominational literature is now rich in interesting material to help the teachers in the Primary grade. It must ever be remembered that the purpose of the church's missionary training in this period is to lay a foundation in thought of God as Father of all, in sympathy for those near at hand who may be helped; in service, by doing things the primary child can do for those he hears about; in missionary zeal, by bringing others into the school.

### 2. Junior

Through the study of geography and history and through reading the world of the Junior child has enlarged over that of his Primary days. The purpose of missionary education in this period is to link this new knowledge with a real spirit of sympathy and friendship. Again we make use of story, prayer, hymn, and gift. Children of this age are very busy with their hands. As they construct an Indian village their imagination weaves about it all the stories the teacher has to tell of the Indian's search for the Great Father and his finding of the Jesus road. In almost every community there will be some alien child of Junior age. A test of the missionary training given by the church will be the attitude of the Junior group toward that child. Juniors will be interested to collect curios and photos, to make scrap-books, dress dolls, visit a near-by mission or settlement, search out boys and girls not in Sunday school and invite them in. There is so much that Juniors may do that the Sunday program of the Junior Department cannot hope to cover it all. Whether the Junior meeting during the week is by classes or as a Junior society the program of their activities will be related to the general activities of the age group to which they belong. Each year denominational study-books for Juniors are prepared dealing with some subject closely related to the subject for adult study. It is of very great advantage to the Junior teacher to have the benefit of current helps in preparing lessons and projects. Missionary stories lend themselves to dramatization which helps the Junior visualize the incident. In the graded missionary material put out by the denominational boards are many delightful, wholesome stories for Juniors. Mothers should be encouraged to use them for bedtime and Sunday reading. Junior boys and girls are old enough to be earning or receiving spending money. They should be taught to practise stewardship, which will include a recognition of God's ownership of all we have and its acknowledgment by a regular and definite giving back to him of his own.

### 3. Intermediate

The Intermediate boy and girl twelve to fourteen years old is at the hero-worshiping age. Now is the time to present Jesus to him as the great ideal and the heroes and heroines of missionary history as illustrations of the power of Jesus to transform and ennoble human life. This is the time for the study of missionary biography. Here again missionary literature is particularly rich in hero stories that make good reading aloud by teacher or mother or that prove fascinating reading to oneself. Intermediates are fond of reading. They are at an age when they enjoy belonging to a club wearing secret insignia, etc. The missionary program of studies and activities gives purpose and continuity to what otherwise might be a short-lived and unrelated association. Preparing Christmas baskets for the local charity organization, making friends with foreigners in the neighborhood, trimming a Christmas tree for a mission school, contributing to the church benevolences, helping with White Cross work are some of the avenues of service open to Intermediates. The dramatization and presentation of a hero story interests the children and may also be a means whereby they may win others to the missionary cause. Within the departmental organization the boys and girls each need their own class or group society or club.

## 4. Senior

By the time young people have reached the early teen years of the Senior Department of the Sunday school they should be ready to get a connected view of missionary history. This is especially important as a complement to their general history study. The expansion of the church, the great medieval and modern heroes of the church, the kind of missionary work they were called upon to do, are suitable subjects for the study of the Senior boy and girl. This period will see the continuation of the Junior societies which have become dear to the children, but they will begin to welcome occasions when boys and girls work together, such as giving a missionary play together or having an occasional program together. Their forms of service will be extensions of those already mentioned for Intermediates. More particular emphasis can be put upon the prayer life and the obligations of stewardship than in the earlier years. In these years the young people should become familiar with the denominational organization and the fields of denominational missionary effort. Again it should be emphasized that all this missionary program building should be a part of an educational whole looking toward a well-rounded Christian life.

## 5. *Young People*

By the time the young people of the church have reached their eighteenth year they should definitely face the question of the why and how of missions. What does a missionary do? Where are missionaries at work? Whom does the Master call to special missionary service? What are the principles of stewardship? There is almost no limit to the variety of missionary service which young people may render. They may teach in mission schools, become leaders of younger groups, arrange social occasions for foreign students, undertake White Cross work, be responsible for a definite part of the church missionary budget, give a missionary play or pageant. These are the years for preparation for special life service. In addition to these general lines of missionary education they may take up in small, special groups the young people's study-book for the year. The denominational missionary programs and literature for young people are interesting, stimulating, thoroughly worth while. When integrated to the whole educational program of the church they ensure a church-membership for tomorrow loyal and informed and ready to serve.

## 6. *Adult*

What sort of missionary education does the adult church-member need? If we might assume an adult who has had the benefit of a religious education in which has been included a program such as we have here outlined, he would naturally progress to a study of the present-day relation of the church and the denomination to the missionary problem; he would try to face the unfinished missionary tasks, to evaluate the missionary significance of current world events, he would take up the study of special home mission fields and separate foreign mission countries.

## An Immediate Missionary Education Program Is Imperative

Unfortunately we have not any considerable number of adults with such a background of training in missionary knowledge, and the missionary task cannot wait the years of their training, so that the church must needs provide an immediate missionary education program for the adult. The Christian church of today is face to face with the disturbing fact that the support of the missionary enterprise depends upon the interest and the contributions of a part of the membership only. It must be that the rest do not know the need of the world for Jesus their only hope. The church is seeking to give her members this knowledge through:

(1) The Missionary Sermon. Even more effective than the occasional sermon is the missionary passion and vision and outlook which is evident in the illustrative material a pastor chooses and in every prayer he voices if he is himself on fire to spread the gospel.

(2) The Church School of Missions. By this is meant a definite series of evenings set aside for missionary study with classes for all ages, usually six evenings and three simultaneous classes. The advantage of this intensive missionary instruction is that it is possible to enlist a large number and to focus their attention upon the missionary problem for this short period.

(3) The Visiting Missionary. It seems hard that our

missionaries must carry the double burden of working on the field and arousing interest at home, but nothing makes so real the missionary appeal as the hearing of one who knows by actual experience whereof he speaks.

(4) Reading Courses. No other cause is so well served by high-grade and interesting literature as is the missionary. Denominational boards offer free leaflets, good magazines, and classified lists of missionary books. There are books for all ages and all tastes, adventure and love stories, travel, history, and biography. To stimulate the interest in reading, various forms of reading contests have been arranged.

(5) Program Meetings. The educational value of a missionary program meeting is not so great as that of a study course, but it is all the education that many church-members receive in this most important subject.

(6) Dramatic Presentations. Through the missionary play or pageant conditions of living other than our own are vividly portrayed, sympathies are aroused, and information is conveyed. We are coming to realize the place of the drama in religious education. There is a great wealth of material for such presentation in the missionary field, and there are now a large number of pageants, plays, dialogues, monologues suited to different ages and different needs.

(7) The Stereopticon. Missionary boards are prepared to furnish stereopticon lectures upon missionary subjects usually for the cost of transportation only. These pictures come carefully packed and marked with a typewritten or printed lecture, so that all the church has to do is to furnish the machine and the reader. This form of education appeals to young and old alike.

(8) Study Classes. In a smaller group it is possible to do intensive study of some special subject. Agreeing upon a country or special subject for the year's study the Protestant denominations publish graded text-books in home and foreign missions. The leading magazines of the country offer articles and stories in line with the study-books of the year. This form of missionary education is building up slowly but surely an intelligent body of Christian people interested in Kingdom affairs, people who cannot be deceived by political propaganda and who have a sympathy wider than the boundaries of their own homes or their own social set.

(9) Discussion Groups and an Occasional Debate. The debate as an educational factor is good in that it compels study on the part of the participants and provokes thought in the hearers. The subject for debate needs, however, to be carefully worded so that no false conclusions shall be reached and no vital subject made to seem either frivolous or purely controversial.

(10) Since the great war two special forms of missionary service have been developed which are important training factors for the adult Christian. One is White Cross Work which uses skill of hand to supply the needs of schools and hospitals. The other is the so-called Christian Americanization Work. Nothing has more severely tested the genuineness of the Christian profession of our church-membership than this opportunity which presents itself to be each one of us real missionaries and through neighborly contacts and the teaching of English point another to the loving Christ.

(11) Training in Stewardship. This is not a division of missionary education any more than of all religious

education, but the needs of the missionary cause have undoubtedly led to a closer study of the Bible teaching concerning money, and this in turn has led the church to realize that its membership must not only be trained in systematic, proportionate giving but in that more inclusive principle of the essential stewardship in which we hold our very selves and all that God has given us.

(12) The adult church-membership of today needs training in the Scope of the Missionary Enterprise. As we have tried to spread the good news of the gospel we have found it necessary to do as Jesus did, to heal the sick and to feed the hungry. The conviction has been borne in upon us that the most we can hope to do on the foreign field is to give the gospel to the few and train them to carry it to the many of their own. Many forms of service have been the direct outgrowth of the desire of the church to obey the command, " Go, disciple."

## Training in the Spirit of Service Must Reach Out Into All the Problems Confronting Society

A modern life as it interprets its own problems, is led inward to the teaching of Jesus; followed outward, brings one to his immediate duty in the modern world. It is not so important to determine where to start as it is to find the Way.[1]

It is a very large order to say to the church that its religious training must include a training in a social interpretation of the gospel message, yet this is exactly where Christ's " follow me " has led us. When the Student Volunteer Movement was organized, young hearts were thrilled with the plea to " Evangelize the World in

[1] " The Social Teachings of Jesus Christ," Francis G. Peabody. By permission of University of Pennsylvania Press.

this Generation." The years passed, and a new generation of young people gathered at Indianapolis for a Student Volunteer Convention. Just as much in earnest, just as ready for sacrifice as the earlier group, they faced new and more difficult barriers to the spread of the gospel, barriers that have been raised or at least perpetuated by Christians themselves. For in a day when what is done in New York is known immediately in Tokio or in Shanghai, the whole non-Christian world is critically examining the fabric of our so-called Christian civilization, and in the light of their adverse criticism these young people and the whole church have been led to examine themselves anew. We have long had prophets among us crying out against our social indifference and ignorance, but the church has been slow to listen to them, believing that by emphasis upon individual salvation and regeneration alone the Kingdom of God would come in. But of late we are beginning to understand that it is quite possible for a man to consider himself a follower of Jesus Christ and yet enjoy comforts and luxuries to provide which other men have labored under unfair and unrighteous conditions. In a word, it is not enough for the church to start individuals on the right road, it must help them find the Way, the Jesus Way of life. As in all educational programs, training in social service must take the form of instruction and expressional activity.

## Training in Service Needs to Be Graded

### 1. The Child

The earliest social institution with which the child comes in contact is his own home. The church can exalt the relation of parent and child and hallow home relationships so that the child's loyalty to home will be strengthened and pride in it increased. This may be done by making church occasions that especially recognize parents, Fathers and Sons, Mothers and Daughters banquets, etc. The child needs training in neighborhood relationships. Our neighbors should be our friends, not our rivals or our enemies. The child moves out from the home into the larger social contacts of school and church. The church can give training in right social attitudes by giving children a part in carrying out the church program and in self-government that will prepare them for their place in a democratic society. It will seek to exalt the heroes of the Cross rather than the heroes of war, and to emphasize the kinship of all peoples regardless of race or color. The training in social activities which the church can give its Primary, Junior, and Intermediate groups is essentially the same as those suggested for training in missionary service. Children may help to keep the streets clean, they may protect a weaker or younger child from gang cruelty. There is a very interesting report of a public-school teacher who found her children discussing the fact that two of their number had typhoid fever, and that some one in that particular family had the disease every year. Following up their interest, the children learned the causes of typhoid fever, the methods of prevention, and made a fly-trap and a covered garbage-pail for the use of this family. They gave their services to help rid the neighborhood of refuse. Theirs was a true missionary and social service.

## 2. *Young People*

By the time our young people reach the high school the church should offer them elementary training in the duties of Christian citizenship, the problems of race relationships, and the causes of war. Biographical studies of the heroes of peace, physicians, teachers, statesmen, explorers, missionaries, are a training in social attitudes invaluable to young life. The young people may undertake leadership in boys' or girls' clubs, services in settlements and mission schools, they may aid in hospital drives, in improved community celebrations. They may undertake to raise the moral standards of a community playground or school environment.

In the young people's department of the church there should be training provided in the Christian social order, international relationships, the relation of the church to social problems, the call to life service in the social field. Young people may be trained in social service by making a survey of social conditions in their neighborhood and undertaking some specific work of social betterment. They should take an active part in local politics. The more clearly the church sees its responsibility to witness for the Master through all of life, the more insistently will she appreciate the necessity for anchoring her young people in a living faith in Jesus as the Saviour of the world.

3. *Adults*

To speak of training the adult membership of the church in social service is to discuss the attitude of the church itself toward these difficult life problems and the place of leadership the church should take. As Dr. Samuel Zane Batten says:

One hope of the gospel is that of a City of God on earth. And we work that this great purpose may be realized. As one approaches this task he is at first appalled by its magnitude and com-

K

plexity. But the more he studies the task, the more clearly he sees it is at bottom a problem of human minds and hearts and wills. It is a question of social knowledge and right attitude of soul: a willingness to pay the price of progress. The only way he [Jesus] knew whereby the world was to be saved was by bearing a cross and giving himself in uttermost service. There is no other way under heaven revealed to men than this way of Christ.

There was a time when it could be said of our civilization that community life and interest centered about the church, and community leadership centered in the church. The church has lost that central place, but it can regain it if it chooses. Many rural churches as well as many churches in crowded city centers have proved that if the church will show its concern for the conditions under which the community lives, its desire to lead in the moral and physical uplift of the neighborhood, its active opposition to injustice and economic wrong, the community will respond by welcoming its help and by listening to its proclamation of the call of Jesus, " Come, follow me."

### Help for the Teacher

Religious education includes training in service. The church looks forward to, proclaims, and labors for the coming of the Kingdom of God. It is therefore vitally interested in the missionary enterprise and in all questions and conditions affecting society. The Christian finds obstacles to service in his own nature and in the nature of the problems involved. The educational program of the church should include graded instruction in missions and social service, also in the actual doing of missionary and social work. Along with this graded work must go a program of immediate education for the present pressing world need.

## Questions for Further Study

1. Make a study of your denominational helps for missionary education.

2. Draw up a plan for reaching all the members of any one age group with training in missionary knowledge and service.

3. How can the church help the family?

# ORGANIZING THE CHURCH SCHOOL

On the great ocean steamer Leviathan a long runway was built for the take-off of an airplane. The experiment proposed to shorten the ocean voyage for mail and passengers by a full day. In spite of difficult weather conditions the experiment was a success.

A runway is needed if the church school is to get under way. The church-school runway is the necessary organization. Let us now consider the machinery which will serve for the launching of the church school. But before we can do that we must be sure we understand what we mean by the term.

## The Church School

In current usage this term has two meanings. It has been applied to the old Sunday school which has continued with the same officers, elected in the same way, and with no changes in organization or program. It has not affected the relations of the school to the other organizations except to make them puzzle over the claim implied in the new name.

The church school as defined by the Education Committee of the International Council of Religious Education is the meaning followed in this discussion. The International Standard for the Church School carries this introductory statement:

The term church school has come into general use with the expanding program of religious education. It is being used increasingly to designate *that organization through which the entire educational program of the church is administered.* The emphasis is laid on the adequacy and unity of the spiritual experience and religious development of the pupil, with only secondary reference to the forms of organization in which that educational experience is realized.

The church school carries out its function through various channels which are but phases of the complete program. Thus there are the Sunday school, vacation church school, week-day church school, missionary societies, young people's clubs and societies, etc. In a church school which has a thoroughly integrated program, these phases provide a cumulative experience which preserves an essential unity in the life of the pupil. In this sense the term church school is used in this standard.

## An Authoritative Church Leadership

If it is the school of the church the offices of leadership must be established by the church, and the appointment must be made by the church for the period and with the powers it shall determine. The common practise of the churches is to invest this leadership in a Board (or Committee) of Religious Education, or a Church Board of Education. The advantage of a Board over a Committee is in permanence, authority, and dignity. A careful nominating committee should present to the church the names of the most competent men and women available without reference to their official relations to any church group. They are to represent the whole church in their individual and collective capacity. The usual period of service is three years, with one-third of the Board elected annually. It is well to keep the Board small, not more than three for the small church with the pastor an ex-officio member.

The Board needs an executive officer. It is usual to call him a Director of Religious Education or the Minister of Education. It is very desirable to secure one who has had professional training in a good department of religious education in a university or seminary. Such a one has prepared for full-time service and must be paid a worthy salary. Where the church is not now able to engage a full-time or even part-time director, an unsalaried position may be created. In some cases the pastor has been named as director until some other could be found and trained. The director is called to a difficult but a delightful task. In addition to his professional knowledge he must have the graces and strengths of leadership. He needs the gracious tact and patience which will enable him to work with all sorts of folks, as well as the initiative and persistence and enthusiasm that refuse to be daunted by any indifference or opposition. Because he deals with methods and organization and technique so largely, his own religious life will be exposed to the danger of becoming mechanized and professional. In some quarters religious education has been brought into disrepute because its champions have been more concerned with form than with substance. He needs to supply fresh inspiration to many volunteer workers, and therefore needs to discover the sources of inward strength for himself. He needs to remind himself as well as his coworkers of the spiritual purpose of it all.

## Leadership Becoming Expert

The failure of many church Boards or Committees of Religious Education to realize the high hopes in their appointment is due in most cases to their failure to qualify

for their office. The position is new, and therefore all
the more difficult to fill. It does not follow that a man
or woman competent in one field of general education or
in one department of religious education, is equipped to
serve as a leader for the church, that is, the whole church
in its educational task. One of the first questions to be
raised by the new board is the question of self-training.
There is hope for a Church Board of Education which
makes confession of its inexpertness and promises the time
and effort necessary to qualify for so significant a leadership.

One pastor secured the consent of the new board to join
a reading class. A book was chosen giving the church
point of view in religious education. Each member was
provided with a copy. They made agreement to read a
chapter in preparation for the weekly study meeting in the
parsonage. Another pastor persuaded the new board to
take one book a week for six weeks and meet with him for
discussion of the material. In the case of another church
the new appointees visited and corresponded with several
church boards of experience who gave them valuable ideas.
One committee resolved itself into a study group and
followed a topical program plan with prepared papers
and discussions.

## Getting the Facts About the Church Situation

Not much progress can be made by a church board in
planning an educational program until it has made a systematic survey of the church. Care should be taken in outlining the information sought in the survey so as to avoid
what is useless for the purposes of the board and to include all the essential facts. Questionnaire forms have

been built, simple and elaborate. Help may be found in the reports of the survey conducted by the Interchurch World Movement, Department of Religious Education, which developed a specialized technique. Several university departments have directed their graduate students in surveys. They have developed suggestive lists of questions and measurements for evaluating their findings. Professor W. C. Bower has given us a helpful volume in " A Survey of Religious Education in the Local Church," with its rather elaborate general schedules for the survey. In " The R. E. D. Book " edited by the Religious Education Department of The American Baptist Publication Society, a simple survey form is suggested.

Schedules of inquiry need to be constructed, adaptable to the local situation. The Board needs to know what organizations connected with the church are carrying on a teaching and training ministry, how many are being reached regularly, what ages, sex, subjects taught, textbooks, if any, educational standards, overlapping. Inquiry needs to be made as to finance, physical equipment, method of selecting officers, competence and training of teachers, relations to general organizations, programs for the church year, etc., etc. It would be well to take time to list the information needed with some care, and then take sufficient time to make the returns accurate. The valuable information thus accumulated can be used best by the Board if put in the form of a large graph and placed on the wall for study.

## An Integrated Program in the Making

The chief purpose of the Church Board of Education is to work toward a balanced and comprehensive church program that shall include all that the church is able to do in the training of childhood, youth, and adults. It will take years, probably many years, to realize this purpose to the full. All that the present Board can do is to make a beginning. How shall the beginning be made? Start with a careful study of the church situation as revealed by the survey. If the graph carries an accurate story of the facts in their relations it will pay to sit down before it in intensive study. Gradually the question will emerge: What can we suggest to these various organization leaders as reasonable steps toward a correlated effort, and the recognition of such common items as may be called items in a church program? Let us consider eight items which a church Board may suggest as the basis of a church scheme.

## 1. Grading by Age Groups

A sharp difficulty in the way of correlation lies in a lack of agreement as to the years included in groups called by the same general names by different organizations, especially among children and young people. In some churches the young people's society includes folks over thirty years of age and folks as young as twelve. A so-called young people's class or missionary society may have in its membership those to whom young people deny the name. Similarly a Junior may be one thing in the Sunday school and another in the missionary group.

The board must face this question for the good of the church and ask, Who belong by right in the age groups, and what age groups shall we recognize? The board should be prepared to suggest age limitations for the groups in every church organization dealing with young

life. The psychology of growing life has established
marked periods. Childhood terminates with adolescence,
which begins at twelve years and closes at twenty-four.
Within childhood, within youth, within adulthood let us
agree upon certain age divisions and expect to limit all
church organizations to these natural groupings.

## 2. Evangelism as a Common Effort

There ought to be no question on the part of any church
worker as to the primacy of the obligation to evangelize.
It ought to be clear that no follower of Christ is exempt
from this command. No society or circle or school or committee or board of the church has a task which is not
subordinate to this supreme duty. Yet in actual practise
the responsibility for the work of evangelism is left on
the shoulders of a few, sometimes left for the lonely
wrestling of the pastor.

Counseling with the pastor as to the division of effort in
the church year and the general plan for the pulpit mes-
sages, and keeping in mind the distinction between the
evangelism of youth and the evangelism of adults, the
board ought to be prepared to bring forward a church
plan of evangelism. This plan will concern itself largely
with the attempt to include the winning of souls to Christ
in the regular educational work. It ought to serve as a
challenge and give specific direction to all. It may include
a plan of training workers for this special task and a period
of earnest prayer.

## 3. Workers and Leaders in Training

Every piece of organized work in the church needs
workers. Many organizations expect to give their workers

all their training in actual service. It would be much better if before beginning work the one who is called to fill an important position had some intelligent conception of the task, of the material to be used, and of the best methods to be employed. It is a loss to the work if a bungling beginner must acquire wisdom through costly experience. Oftentimes such a beginner becomes discouraged and resigns. It frequently happens that a valuable leader is lost, and no provision has been made for preparing a successor.

The training of teachers and workers and leaders is difficult. Everybody who is worth including on a staff is busy. While they confess to their need of training they do not see where they can find the time. This includes our young people, whether in school or in business. Somebody must feel so strongly the evils of a lack of training for Christian work that their enthusiasm for proper training will overcome all obstacles. It would be of advantage if the champion of training could speak for the whole church and all its active groups.

Plainly this need is one for the early consideration of a church board. Some plan must be devised of sharpening the sense of need for training. Probably more than one group is suffering because its leadership has fallen into a rut. The best way to condemn obsolete methods and secure progress is through a general informational and training occasion.

The Board should not confine itself to one form of training. It must be ready to suggest a variety of efforts to be made at different times. It will consider an Educational Week when the church will be asked to give every evening and some afternoons to training-classes, conferences, demonstrations, exhibits, and inspirational platform meetings. There are some general principles founded in human nature or the nature of the church and religion, or the common material of instruction we all must use, that are significant for all engaged in any form of church work. Then there are specialized courses and discussions which have meaning for selected groups. Both kinds of training-classes must be provided.

Another plan which has been worked successfully is Church Night or Night Church School. For a limited period, say of six or ten weeks, the pastor asks his people to give one night a week to their church. The whole evening is spent in sociability, training, and devotion. One or two periods may be used in two or more simultaneous classes before the closing devotional period or church prayer-meeting.

With the help of the denominational or State specialist a Standard Training School may be arranged. We may have a Training School or Institute designed for young people's work. The board may strengthen the teacher-training class of the Sunday school, or build up individual correspondence or reading courses. Through agencies outside the church a training-school may be set up in the community, or a convention and conference with training features arranged or summer assemblies and summer training-schools may invite our church workers. Part of the responsibility of the board will be to select delegates and representatives, and secure their attendance. Care must be had by the board lest some form of necessary training work be neglected, such as the preparation of leaders for missionary education, the vacation school, organized play, and the ministry of music.

## 4. *The Vacation Church School*

Dr. A. H. Gage, in " How to Conduct a Church Vacation School," reports a young woman who went to her pastor one day and said, " Pastor, do you know what I have been thinking our church ought to do this summer? "

" I do not know what you have been thinking, but I know what I have been praying that we might do."

She said, " I have been studying up the work of the daily vacation Bible school and believe we ought to have a school in our church."

" Why, that is just what I have been praying for," he said.

She became principal of the school, the first in her church and the first in her community, and ministered to over three hundred boys and girls that summer.

This incident repeated by scores of vacation-school pioneers illustrates how the movement began as a result of individual efforts. The vacation school has passed through its experimental stages and has established itself as a regular part of the church's ministry in religious education. It has demonstrated that boys and girls welcome interesting occupation during the long summer vacation, that young people home from college and others are willing to offer their services, that a uniquely varied and appealing program can be provided, that the unused church building can be made a community blessing, that an attendance can be drawn from homes not previously related to a Protestant church, that it builds the church into the good-will of the neighborhood, and that it doubles the meager time devoted to the religious training of primaries, juniors, and intermediates.

It ought not take a church board long to discover that a vacation school is an integral part of the church school, and that it would be unfortunate if a separate organization grew up to administer it. A responsibility of the board is to see to it that the finances are raised, superintendent and teachers selected, curriculum determined, the conduct of the school supervised, and a report made to the church constituency by a graduation, exhibit of handwork, demonstration, or other service interesting to the public.

## 5. *The Week-day Church School*

Some years ago Dr. H. F. Cope made a careful study of religious instruction in the city of Chicago, visiting nearly one thousand church schools of practically all faiths. His conclusion was that of the total number of children between five and eighteen only one in five was receiving any regular instruction in religion in any kind of school or church, whether Protestant, Catholic, Hebrew, or any other. Under Dr. W. S. Athearn the Interchurch World Movement surveyed " sample " American communities including a typical State. His conclusions was that over 27,000,000 persons under twenty-five years of age belonging to the Protestant group are not in any Sunday school.

The limited number of children reached by Protestant instruction, the limited period of instruction on Sunday for those that are reached, and the irregular attendance of those enrolled are the cause of the agitation for week-day instruction. The movement among the churches has been assisted by public-school leaders who are asking whether the secularizing of public education has not contributed to an increase of lawlessness and crime. School boards which have faced their responsibility for moral

training are usually ready to give the churches every en-
couragement in any reasonable plan of relating religious
training to the general education of the child.

Dr. T. S. Young, one of the leaders in the movement,
estimates that more than one thousand communities have
taken steps toward the organization of week-day religious
schools. These schools are using released time granted
the children on the parents' request by the Board of Education or are using such free time as is left in the week.
The week-day school may be organized by a single church,
or by churches in cooperation or by a Community Board
of Religious Education. The type which best secures
cooperative action and preserves the integrity of the individual church school is the denominational-community type.

If a week-day school has been established, the Church
Board of Education should seek an official relationship to
its administration. If no effort has been made to canvass
the matter, it becomes a concern of the church board.
Speaking for the whole church the board may confer with
representatives of other churches as to a community movement. It should be officially represented in any community
organization. It will undertake to make the week-day
school an integral part of its own church school.

## 6. *Missionary Education*

Stacy R. Warburton says, in " Making a Missionary
Church " :

The mission of every church is the mission of Christ and the
apostles—to give the gospel to the whole world. That means that
every church is a missionary organization. All the world is its
field. Its responsibility to one part of that world field is no greater
than to another. If it is under obligation to make its community

Christian, it has equal obligation to make China and India and Africa and South America Christian.[1]

At least one member of the Church Board of Education should be chosen because of competence and conviction in the field of missionary education. This member may well be the chairman of a Church Committee on Missionary Education which submits all its educational plans to the approval of the Church Board of Education. Since missionary education is so important to the whole church and its training work, it would be well for the board to give an entire evening meeting to a consideration of the plans prepared by the Committee on Missionary Education. This Committee should study carefully the needs of each age group, what is now being done to enlist all the group, the material issued by the denominational department of missionary education, and frame a comprehensive and practicable plan for the consideration of the church board who will make it a part of the general educational program of the church. The execution of the plan as approved may well be placed in the hands of the Committee on Missionary Education.

Missionary education should be kept distinct from missionary promotion which seeks an immediate offering. This responsibility belongs elsewhere, on other church officers. Missionary education belongs to the educational leadership which is seeking to build a unified educational organization for the whole church.

Supplementing the detailed plans for each department which include mission-study classes, program meetings, missionary stories, pageants, plays, White Cross work, reading courses, etc., the church should give itself to an intensive consideration of its missionary obligations at one period of the year. The School of Missions affords this opportunity. Many churches are now committed to a series of church nights in the autumn when general training-courses, Biblical, technical, and missionary are given, and to a Church School of Missions in the spring when the exclusive emphasis is on missionary information and inspiration.

## 7. *Social Education*

Dr. Samuel Zane Batten wrote in " Building a Community ":

The purpose of Christ is not individual alone but social also. He comes to save men that they may become children in God's family and serve in his kingdom. He does not save men out of relations but in relations. The central idea of Christianity is the Kingdom of God; and this Kingdom in Christ's conception never means anything less than a divine human society on earth.

One test of the total educational work of a church must be, Have you made the individual a better member of society? Religious education ought to be bringing in a better family, a better community, a better State, a better Church, a better industrial order, better international relations. Is the church training resulting in social attitudes, social habits, and social ideals? As the teacher of morals and religion the church must be interested in public education, in law enforcement, in the lessening of crime and the care of criminals, in movements for reform, in the standards of commercialized amusements, in charity and welfare administration, etc. Part of the responsibility of

L

the board which plans for the whole church in education is to make sure that social education finds its proper place.

## 8. Teaching Stewardship

The relative failure of the churches to realize their splendid programs for missionary advance has compelled a study of the causes. It has become evident to our church leaders that we have failed in an understanding and practise of stewardship. Dr. F. A. Agar says, "If the world is to be won to the Kingdom of Jesus Christ, more time, energy, talent, and personality as well as money are required from those who love him and desire to serve him."

Training in stewardship must begin with the young child and be carried consistently through the curriculum of the church. This is too big an affair for any limited group. It is a concern of the Church Board of Education.

## The Advisory Council of Religious Education

A famous English critic of America says that we have a weakness for voluntary organizations. Some wag tells of a shipwrecked company discovered on a lonely island. The two Englishmen had not spoken to each other, for they had not been introduced. The two Scotchmen had incorporated a bank and were holding all the currency in sight. The two Americans had organized a Boosters Club and Rotary, and had divided the offices.

There is a tendency in church work to overorganize. Some enthusiastic soul goes off to a convention or conference of some sort and gets a brand-new idea. Straightway he goes back to the home church, arouses a group of well-meaning people to the proper pitch of excitement, and lo, a club or circle or some other combination is formed, organized, and properly officered. As a result of our laxity in permitting propaganda from general movements to invade the local church we have a conglomerate of organizations claiming the name of the church, but without definite relations to each other or to the church.

The Advisory Council of Religious Education is not an additional piece of machinery but a means of simplifying what we now have. It is not another regular meeting and another set of duties, but is an informal gathering of the present leadership of the various active organizations to counsel with the Church Board of Education. When the board has completed its study of the church situation, and has made a tentative statement for itself of those items it is prepared to recommend as the first steps toward a church program, it issues an invitation for the first meeting of the Advisory Council.

The Advisory Council is constituted for a brief service because this seems to be the best way of meeting the difficulties of correlation. Each group has hitherto worked in almost complete isolation and independence of every other group. It has developed a group loyalty, sometimes an intense loyalty about its name, and is jealous of its prestige and rights. The tactful leadership of the Church Board will make a list of the significant groups, assign a proper number of representatives to each, and fix a time of meeting.

At the opening of the meeting the purpose of the Advisory Council should be explained. It is not a legislative body but a meeting for friendly counsel. The board is seeking to correlate, and ultimately to unify all the educational work. It desires to take the first steps in partnership with the leaders who have grown up in the work of the church. To this end a survey has been made of the work which is being done, and an interesting graph has been prepared, which the Advisory Council can assist in making accurate. Does the graph represent faithfully the work and program of your organization? After sufficient time for study the various executives will be ready to make any necessary changes or additions.

The graph will enable the board to make clear the need of proper relationships, the points of overlapping, the gaps not provided for, and the need of a general church program which all will recognize. It is now prepared to bring forward its suggestions of a few items which all are asked to include in the work of their group as a common church program. Such items from among the eight listed above or other items will be considered. The meeting, under the gentle guidance of the Church Board ought to resolve to do a certain number of things as a church.

The council should be called together when the need arises and not regularly. In the beginning it will need more frequent meetings than later. Its discussions carried on in a friendly constructive spirit ought to deepen the church consciousness and define more clearly the church task. The members of the council will expect to carry the common plan back to their own groups and secure for it favorable consideration.

### An Adequate System of Finance

"Hear the pennies dropping" is no longer sung in a well-regulated Beginners or Primary department. Many churches are still practising it, however. The religious training of their children depends upon the pennies they bring. So important has education become for the community, whether of city or country, that citizens tax themselves more heavily for the school than for any other item in the budget.

The necessary educational work of the church ought to be recognized by the church budget. All the proper and regular expenses of any essential church group are church expenses. They are provided in one form or another by church people. Ultimately these expenses ought to enter a common budget for which the church makes itself responsible. All bills regularly approved will then be paid from the church treasury.

The Church Board must come to a study of finances. It will discover that some important work is being limited while some other work is favored by generous support. An adult class may have more than it needs in its treasury while a children's department is neglected. It may also learn that the present system of giving develops class and club attachments at the expense of church loyalty. An increasing number of churches are using one duplex envelope for all the organizations of the church. The church budget is built to meet all the need of the home church, including religious education. A missionary and benevolent budget is built to express the generous outreach of the church. A canvass is made at the beginning of the fiscal year for pledges for both current expenses and missions from the entire church constituency. Each one who pledges receives his packet of duplex envelopes which he may use at any service.

## Housing, Furnishings, and Supplies

The modern school is demanding a physical equipment much more elaborate than was dreamed of a generation ago. This is true of the high school, university, and technical school. It is not strange that the church school should feel the need of a building adapted to school work. This urge is the more insistent because the builders of churches had little appreciation of sociability, recreation, and education up to within a few years. So generally is this true that as soon as church leadership is aroused to reorganize the work of religious education it makes a systematic survey of the present building, its main rooms, its seating arrangements, its blackboards, its maps, its musical instruments, its hymn-books, its library facilities, its pictures, its materials for cutting, pasting, coloring, molding, etc., etc. In short, some one is appointed to read everything the best books say about equipment, visit well-furnished church schools, check up the physical needs of the home church school, and report a list of recommendations to the Church Board, with estimated expense. Some of this expense may be carried in the church budget this year with the expectation of adding further items next year. It may be that the church ought to build an educational building. In that case consultation should be had with the denominational department of church architecture.

### Records

One State has an elaborate system of checking up on autoists. When a traffic officer finds a transgressor of regulations such as those concerning traffic signals, speeding, or breaking parking rules, he calls for the driver's license card and punches the item noting the offense, " W " for warning and two " A's " for arrests. Each driver's record becomes significant.

The faithful record of every member and officer of the

church school is significant for the individual, and significant to the church as a measurement of progress.  The
Indiana Survey reported:

> The only data on pupils which the Sunday school authorities in
> all schools regarded as sufficiently important to record are the
> full name of the pupil and his absence from class.  Nine out of ten
> of the Sunday schools record these facts.  About half the schools
> make a record of the residence of the pupil and the date of the
> pupil's birth.

Such carelessness in the important matter of record keeping is inexcusable.  We ought to have an individual record
card in the secretary's file, containing the essential facts
about the pupil, his family, his regularity, his class marks,
promotions, date of joining church, special service, etc.
We need a careful class and departmental record.  This
also applies to all the young people's and adult work.  We
need careful quarterly and annual reports if we are to
check up on our gains and losses.

## Pupil Partnership

The school of democracy must be the pupil's school.
It must assist him toward self-reliance, initiative, self-
discipline, and social organization.  It is not so much what
is done for him as what he learns to do for himself.
Studied effort must be made to relate him to the school
management.  He ought to be represented in a Student
Council of the School, and in the department councils.
He needs to think and feel, " My church, my class, my
club, my bunch."  It is worth while having a school or society song, a cheer, an emblem, colors, a rallying cry or
slogan, anything that appeals to the imagination, which will
weave into group experiences and develop sentiment.

Modern education insists upon expressional work. Good teaching and wise leadership wins pupil participation. In view of the autocratic organization of the school which we have inherited and of the traditions of Sunday-school teaching which made it a sermon or a lecture, it is necessary to ask about our general educational scheme, Are we making the most of pupil activity?

## Supervision

It is a practise of conventions and congresses to pass pious resolutions and adjourn. It is a habit we have in church work of making splendid plans which look fine on the typewritten sheet, then going home to forget all about them. It will not be difficult for the Church Board to construct a splendid educational scheme. Somebody must be held responsible for following up plans and keeping contact with those who are made responsible for special pieces of work. Those who are charged with supervision ought to be released from teaching or administration.

## Interrelations

No man liveth unto himself. No church can thrive as a hermit. In its educational ministry the church is related to the home, to the public school, to the public library, to the public playground, but especially to other churches which are carrying on a similar ministry. In its denominational affiliation it is related to the board or society to which religious education has been committed. It is related interdenominationally to the churches of the community as they seek to advance the cause of religious education. It is also related to the International Council of Religious Education, to the auxiliary State council, and to the World's Sunday School Association. It is the business of the church-school leadership to make vital and helpful all these rich relationships.

## Help for the Teacher

The church school is the organization through which the entire educational program of the church functions. It must therefore be an integral part of the church organization. The church usually appoints a committee or board for this purpose, defines its function and powers. Very probably the members of this board will need to prepare themselves by reading or study for their task, they must make an educational survey of the church, put their findings in a graph, suggest gradual changes to effect a proper grading, common evangelical effort, training-courses for leaders, the vacation and week-day school, missionary and social education, adequate financing and equipment, proper records, and a method of supervision. The board needs the cooperation of a representative council, it needs the active enlistment of the pupils, it needs to strengthen its denominational and interdenominational relations.

## Questions for Further Study

1. Draw up a plan for a Church Board of Education and an Advisory Council, defining duties, relations, and membership of each.

2. Learn from denominational headquarters what help is available for leadership training, and discuss what plan will best suit the needs of your church.

3. Plan the organization of one department of a church

school according to the definition of the school in this chapter.

4. Define the duties and powers of a Director of Religious Education.

## A Sample Constitution

Dr. George L. White was asked whether the principles sketched in this chapter on organization were armchair dreams or actually usable. He replied by sending the following with permission to print:

The First Baptist Church of Los Angeles, in preparing to enter its new million dollar equipment, voted to request its Board of Religious Education to work out a plan of organization and a constitution, which, in a clear, definite manner would set forth the objects of the school, the responsibilities in executive leadership, the relationships of various cabinets, councils, societies, and individuals, the plan of finance, and the relationship of the school organization to the church.

The report submitted by the Board of Religious Education was adopted and the following articles placed in the church constitution and a new constitution written for the church school.

### EXTRACTS FROM THE CHURCH CONSTITUTION

SECTION 3, ARTICLE III. There shall be a Church Board of Religious Education, composed of the Pastor (or Pastors) and the Director of Religious Education, who shall serve ex-officio, and seven members to be elected by the church; of these seven members two shall be elected each year for a period of two years, and three, who shall be nominated by the Church Board of Religious Education, shall be elected each year for a period of one year.

SECTION 6, ARTICLE IV. *Duties of the Church Board of Religious Education.* The Church Board of Religious Education shall have full responsibility for the administration of all of the educational work of the church. It shall consider and, in cooperation with the Finance Committee of the Church, have full authority in all matters pertaining to the financial management of the church school, and shall represent the church in the direction of all of its educational interests.

## Extracts from the School Constitution

Article I. This School shall be known as "The First Baptist Church School," of Los Angeles, California.

Section 2, Article II. The Church School shall unify in its organization and operation all educational interests of the Church, including the Sunday School, Young People's Work, Teacher Training, Missionary Education, Vacation Schools, Week-day Religious Education, and all other lines of study, instruction, recreation, and service included in a comprehensive and balanced program of Christian education. No scheme of training or organization for educational purposes shall be promoted within the Church School without the approval of the Church Board of Religious Education.

### Article IV

Section 1. The Church School shall be the Church itself at work in education and every part of the School shall be responsible to the Church through its Board of Religious Education.

Section 2. The Church Board of Religious Education shall have full responsibility for the administration of all of the educational work of the church.

Section 3. *Divisions.* The School shall have three divisions, namely, the Children's, Young People's, and Adult's.

Section 4. *Departments.* (a) The Children's Division shall have four Departments: namely, Cradle Roll, Beginners, Primary, and Juniors. (b) The Young People's Division shall have three Departments, Junior High School, Senior High School, and Older Young People. (c) The Adult Division shall have three Departments, Men's, Women's, and Extension.

Section 5. Each Department shall include all educational, recreational, and social interests within the Church adapted to pupils of the age of those in that Department.

Section 6.  Each organized class, society, and club, with the assistance and advice of the Division Cabinet, shall adopt its own form of organization, provided that it is in accord with this Constitution.

## Article V

Section 3.  There shall be a Director of Religious Education, nominated by the Church Board of Religious Education, and elected by the Church, who shall work under the Church Board of Religious Education, and who shall preside at all general meetings of the School and of the Teachers and Officers.

Section 4.  The following officers, as needed, shall be appointed by the Church Board of Religious Education and shall act as assistants to, and work under the direction of, the Director of Religious Education.  Each shall have the privilege of enlisting and appointing his own assistants as needed.  These officers shall be as follows:

(1) A Director of Records—who shall act as the general secretary of the school.

(2) A Director of Finance—who shall also act as Treasurer.

(3) A Director of Reading—who shall have charge of the library and reading-room of the church school, and who shall encourage helpful reading on the part of the officers, teachers, and pupils.

(4) A Director of Publicity.

(5) A Director of Grading and Pupil Classification.

(6) A Director of Teacher and Leadership Training.

(7) A Director of Worship.

(8) A Director of Music.

(9) A Director of Missions.

(10) A Director of Evangelism.

(11) A Director of Recreation.

(12) A Director of Community Service.

Section 5.  There shall be three (3) Superintendents; one of the Children's Division, one of the Young People's Division, and one of the Adult Division.  All Superintendents shall act as assistants to the Director of Religious Education and as the administrative officers of their several divisions.  They shall be members ex-officio of all councils and committees appointed within their respective divisions.

SECTION 6. There shall be principals of all Departments who shall act as assistants to their Division Superintendents, and as administrative officers in their several Departments.

SECTION 1, ARTICLE VI. There shall be an Advisory Council of the Church School, which shall be composed of representatives from all Divisions, Departments, and interests of the School. It shall consist of the following persons: The Pastor or Pastors, the Director of Religious Education, the Church Board of Religious Education, the Division Superintendents, the Department Principals, all Secretaries, Directors, and Teachers, and all presidents, chairmen, or heads of organized classes, societies, and clubs. This Council, as its name indicates, shall be advisory and shall never assume executive functions.

SECTION 1, ARTICLE VIII. The Church School budget shall be a part of the Annual Budget of the Church. At least four (4) weeks before the annual business meeting of the Church, a committee consisting of the Church Board of Religious Education, the Director of Finance, and the three (3) Division Superintendents, shall determine an itemized budget for the Church School, which shall be recommended to the Church through its Finance Committee for consideration, adjustment, and approval, at the annual meeting of the Church.

# THE SUPREME SPIRITUAL EMPHASIS

To her consternation mother discovered there was nothing in the house for dinner, and the time was painfully short. Jack was ordered to leave his play and hasten to the village for meat. Active-minded Jack immediately thought of a number of things the gang needed in the village and of several interesting stunts that venturesome boys could enjoy in that same village. Mother's voice had hardly died away before the ready gang was organized for the expedition. It was time to sit down at table before they reappeared with a most exciting report and with string, nails, "suckers," a whistling top, a baseball glove, but without the meat.

## Religious Education Is Being Criticized

It is said that religious education is doing many interesting things not done before, but it comes home without the meat. The old doubters who were satisfied with ancient methods called it a modern fad when it struggled for recognition two decades ago. It may be expected that some of them will remain critics without any friendliness of spirit. More significant is the criticism of sincere friends of the movement. Recently in a well-known religious weekly Dean Shailer Mathews wrote an article under the striking heading "Religious Education—Beware!" Dean Mathews was associated with Dr. William Rainey Harper in organizing the Religious Education

Association a quarter of a century ago. His warning is all the more significant because he has continued an active leader in the movement. He says that religious education is in danger of minimizing the church, of hiding God behind a smoke screen of psychology, of reviving the atomistic treatment of the Scriptures, and of overemphasizing technique.

Probably every member of the teacher-training class has heard critics, informed and uninformed, pronounce upon the new methods and principles which are generally classified as religious education. It would be interesting to listen to a symposium of reported comment which had been brought in by the class. If there is a danger, as Dean Mathews asserts, to the movement, to the church, and to religion, we ought to give heed to honest critics who are seeking to point out faults. Let us attempt a summary of the most significant of these criticisms as they have come from many quarters.

## *1. The Conceit of Professionalism*

This is directed toward those who have taken training-courses in a recognized institution primarily, but also includes those who have taken any training-work, especially for credit. Pastors have quoted of recent graduates, " A little knowledge is a dangerous thing." One pastor reviews the directors of religious education who have been on the church staff with this comment, " They had the ex-cathedra spirit in so pronounced a degree that they resented all criticism." In conventions and conferences of trained workers it is all too common to draw a line between us who know and those who do not know. The necessity of condemning improper practises may give us a superior

material of social living. But we must not overlook the
first great command to love God with all our heart and
soul and mind and strength. Equally must we know communion with him or our social living is incomplete, and
our religious education is neither religion nor education.

## 6. Undermining the Authority of the Scriptures

This criticism comes from those who object to nature
lessons, church history since the completion of the canon,
missionary expansion, and all other extra-Biblical material.
That objection is too narrow if the Bible is kept in the first
place. We must take account of the charge if we find
we have so overloaded the curriculum as to overshadow
*the* Book, or if we are handling the Bible for its literature
and history while losing sight of its unique purpose. This
library of books has grown out of religious experience and
must contribute to religious experience, or it fails of its
chief end.

## 7. Overemphasis on the Intellectual

This is the objection of those who question whether religion can be taught. It may presuppose an overemphasis
on the emotional or on the practical. That there is an
intellectual factor in every balanced religious life all will
admit. The Christian man needs considerable information,
needs to formulate his own convictions, needs a serviceable
mental equipment to understand a tangled situation and
apply his Christian principles. That is not all he needs.
That is the easiest portion to supply him in religious training. Every Sunday-school teacher is tempted to follow
the line of least resistance, teach facts, and let it go at that
to the neglect of heart culture.

## 8. Class Exclusiveness

In the columns of magazines carrying educational advertising, not infrequently schools commend themselves on the ground they are catering exclusively to a favored few. They are select schools. They pride themselves on the limits placed on membership and the care with which they choose and refuse. By placing too high requirements upon school equipment and accepted teachers, religious educators may in effect so seriously limit the school as to make it undemocratic. The public school takes pride in its service for all the children of all the people. The church school must reflect its Master's concern for all sorts and conditions of men, while it struggles to do better work for each pupil.

## 9. A Lack of Passion

A very serious complaint against any preacher or religious teacher is that he does not feel the mighty truth he discusses so glibly. If the teaching were of the trivial affairs of life, no surprise would be expressed. Since the teacher is seeking to awaken a passionate devotion to his Lord in the heart of the pupil, it is all the more necessary that he have a depth of conviction. Here is an ever-present danger that needs to be guarded against. Let us ask later in this lesson how we may cultivate passion in teaching.

## 10. Limiting Education to the Young

Most Sunday schools are made up of children and young people. The institution still suffers from its early name, Infants' School. General education stops training with adolescence. If a man of thirty is found among the college students it causes remark. It is not so with the church school. We expect to retain a name on the membership roll from the cradle to the grave. If any school fails to attempt an Adult Department it has missed the spirit and genius of religious education.

### Results to Be Expected

Some results elude the annual report. These intangible quantities are the very purpose of our work. Now and again church-school leadership should list these elusive values and seek a general judgment as to the gains and losses under each. Let us attempt to name some of the more important results that a good school will produce.

### *1. Church Loyalty and Attractiveness*

The church school ought to be making a great contribution to the church life in strengthening church ties and in winning the good-will of the neighborhood. A good school will exalt the church, guard the good name of the church, honor the church leadership, and strengthen affection and devotion to the church. Especially will the school express the friendly, welcoming spirit of the church. The fellowship of the church will become attractive to strangers, so that new people will be drawn irresistibly to both church and school.

### *2. Numbers Finding Their Saviour and Growing Beautiful in Character*

The school is not a camp-meeting nor a high-pressure evangelistic campaign. But it would be strange if a church school carried on year after year and no boy or girl were led to the greatest discovery of youth. It ought to cause a serious questioning of officers and teachers and workers if religious education in their hands does not quietly and happily introduce seeking hearts to the Lord of Life and Beauty. His Spirit at work in hearts may be expected to mold plastic lives into lives of beauty.

### 3. Sincerity in Worship

It is possible to tame a wild, turbulent, irreverent company of street youngsters who have no respect for the mission house and no appreciation of the meanings of worship. We will not expect to reach a model worship service in one year, but we do expect gains in better order, quietness, a spirit of prayer, singing with understanding, and a growing sense of the presence of God.

### 4. Missionary Interest

It may be that we have more than the ordinary obstacles to combat, such as indifference, prejudice against foreigners, fear of it costing something, ignorance. It may take harder work in some churches than in some others. Surely we may confidently expect that missionary education faithfully carried out will produce human sympathy, a desire to help even at a sacrifice, and a real concern for the peoples without opportunity of hearing the gospel message.

### 5. Desire for Training

We ought to expect that many young people will make choices of life work from motives of Christian service under the influence of the church school. We will expect that many young people will be turned to church work at the call of their Master. There ought to be such an exalting of Christian work that candidates for training are coming forward. Such a dignifying of service for the King, such a presentation of its exacting demands as the church school can make, ought to stir present workers and leaders to desire more training.

### 6. *Stewardship Expressed in Generous Giving*

Many worthy enterprises of the church are failing because Christian people spend on their luxuries but are niggardly toward the church and Kingdom work. Many boys and girls spend considerable sums in the aggregate on ice-cream, movies, and other indulgences, but feel little concern about giving as determined by Christian principles. May not the church school expect a deepening sense of Christian stewardship and a generous proportion of all income devoted to the Lord?

### 7. *Quickening of Conscience*

There are mighty evils, organized and entrenched, toward which the community seems indifferent. Ethical questions arise in every life, but especially with youth who must establish precedents for themselves by doing things for the first time. The church school will have much to do in fixing the moral tone of the entire church. Are we cultivating a sensitive conscience toward social evils and inculcating a moral thoughtfulness as the individual faces his personal questions?

### 8. *Social Vision*

Our modern complex life sometimes arouses the desire to flee from it all into the simplicities of a hermit existence. That is impossible. Young people must be trained in their social obligations. Men and women must have their sympathies broadened beyond narrow family or parish or race or sectarian restrictions. They must grow into understanding and conviction of Christ entering all human relations. Are we giving this vision?

## Stumbling-blocks in the Way

Idealism would soon become realism if it were not for human nature. It's a strange mixture, this human nature of ours, often joining together purest aspiration and sordid motive, noble profession and base practise, ready promises with an equally ready forgetting. If we are to make our church school the spiritual power it ought to be, we must remove the stumbling-blocks in the way, tactfully, patiently, firmly.

### *1. Prayerlessness*

" Paul may plant, and Apollos water, but God giveth the increase." Paul and Apollos were expert workmen. They would rank high among the graduates of any training-course. Their work would have been a fizzle and a bitter disappointment except for God's blessing. Does the church school expect God's blessing, or does it feel quite competent to do all that is necessary without him? Is any provision made for waiting on God in prayer?

### *2. Inconsistent Living*

Boys and girls turn sharp eyes on teachers and school leaders. In the sophistry of the transgressor certain lapses in moral living may be forgiven a man who is doing a good deal for the church. Young critics know no such leniency of judgment toward one prominent in religious work. Christ warned of the seriousness of being a stumbling-block to the weak. " It were better for him that a millstone were hanged about his neck and he cast into the sea, than that he should offend one of these little ones." We ought not to continue in leadership one whose life is known to be untrue.

### 3. Envy and Jealousy

These are ugly green monsters who do much harm. The church school asks men and women of different temperaments to work together on most intimate terms. Some must appear on the platform and be in the public eye. A too frequent praise may become public flattery, while some worker equally faithful has been overlooked. There are many opportunities for jealousy but that devilish spirit must be crucified as soon as it appears.

### 4. Cliques

It is natural for us to like congenial folks. If we are asked to do a piece of work it is natural to ask the help of our friends. Before we are aware we may have built up a self-contained group of kindred spirits and shut ourselves out from association with others, when we know that the great Head of the Church is opposed to all snobbishness and special privilege in his church. We need to be reminded frequently of his desire for a friendly association which includes everybody.

### 5. Unwillingness to Serve

Jesus told a story of two boys whose father bade them work in his vineyard. One said, " No," and repented, while the other said, " Yes," but did not go. The Lord asks volunteer service. It is a very sad situation when the church school cannot do its proper work because young people and older people are busy with so many other things they have no time to give to the Master of their lives.

### 6. Bossism

Every human enterprise, and especially a school, needs strong executive ability. It is not possible to make a strong class or society or department or club without a strong leader. Strength may be confused with egotism and self-assertion. There is a better strength than that of the autocrat. There is no place in Christian work for a boss who leaves fellow workers undeveloped through depriving them of independence and initiative. " Whosoever will be chief among you, let him be your servant."

### 7. Unreliability

School work calls for regularity. This is particularly true of a school whose pupils come voluntarily. A class is soon lost if the teacher is not faithful. The cause of haphazard work may usually be found in undependability.

### 8. Failure of Faith

In Pilgrim's Progress the author tells of Christian finding lions in the way. Courage overcame fear as at the call of Watchful he went forward boldly to discover the lions were chained. Not a few superintendents and presidents and directors and Church Boards of Education find lions in the way. A spirit of hopelessness may settle down on the whole enterprise. In such a situation some one must be found to raise the battle-cry, " The sword of the Lord and of Gideon!" It was a lonely but iron-hearted prophet who said, " They that are for us are greater than those who are against us."

## Cultivating the Spiritual

How shall we meet the criticisms of religious education, how may we realize the results which are rightfully expected, and how may all stumbling-blocks be removed from the way? Plainly, the answer is by cultivating the spiritual possibilities of the church school. There are certain features connected with the work of a school of religion which are designed to safeguard us from a careless materialism.

### 1. Preparation of Heart for Leading in Worship

We have seen that the responsibility for directing the public worship of God is a weighty matter. It must be prepared for carefully as to program, meeting-room, instrument, hymn-books, etc. The most important preparation is made in the heart of the leader. The spirit of worship is contagious. When Moses comes down the mountain with radiant face all Israel knows he has been in audience before the Ineffable Majesty.

### 2. Devotional Bible Study

Workers in the church school, teachers and leaders, have a great gain in the material of instruction. The first application of the truths studied should be made in the study. If we can persuade our teaching staff to make Bible study devotional first of all, the battle for a spiritually minded school is all but won. Give the Bible a chance, and it searches the heart's deeps, purifying, ennobling, making Christlike.

### 3. Friendship for Jesus' Sake

The church school cannot maintain itself without
friendship. One of the choicest opportunities comes to
the teacher. Equally wonderful is the chance of making
friends within the group of church young people. Friendships may degenerate into selfish satisfactions. It will
materially help the school keep first things first if these
school and church friendships can all be for Jesus' sake.
We long for our friend nothing less than the wealth which
Jesus has to give.

### 4. A Personal Religious Ministry

In the days of " revival " meetings it came to be believed
that no soul could be saved except at stated seasons. But
crises come in individual lives at different times and under
different circumstances. Fortunate is that church school
whose workers are on the watch for souls. No one needs
to tell teacher that John is ready to be talked to about
personal salvation. No matter how busy that teacher may
be, so important a matter must not be neglected, or the
chance will be lost. It will be true also in the case of
one who strays away. He has been missed from his regular place in the church school, it is known that evil associates are enticing him, but a friend of his hunts him out
and wins him back. Personal work done in the name of
Christ quickens faith and love as nothing else can.

### 5. The Fall Retreat

This does not mean a retreat in the face of the enemy.
It is not that kind of a retreat. It is the gathering of the
group of workers apart to pray and plan. Before the

summer vacations break up many churches look forward
to the September meeting of the workers, often in a quiet
spot at some distance from the church, for meditation, devotion, and reconsecration, as well as for such a planning
together that all may understand what is expected of them.
The wise pastor will make use of this unique occasion to
bring home to all how helpless we are without God and
how ready he is to meet our need. He will also make room
for a rededication to God of every teacher and leader and
worker.

With this lesson our study of the church in its relation
to the church school comes to an end. We have considered why the church must teach, the efforts of the
church in the past to teach, and the confusion of plans
in the church today because of the many organizations
doing their work independently of each other. The time
has come for the church to define its aim in religious
education and to survey the means available for realizing
its aim. Special attention must be given to the curriculum
of the church school including its training in worship, in
social living, and through service. After a consideration
of these important factors in a church scheme of religious
education, we studied the organization of an enterprise
large enough to be called the church school. Finally, we
backed away from our subject far enough to get a perspec-
tive and discover its chief characteristic, that which gave
it significance and value. We have seen that the outstanding fact in any church school worthy the name is its
religious character. Having given our serious and prayerful study to this tremendous subject, the obligation rests
upon each one of us to strive to make the church school
what it ought to be.

## Help for the Teacher

Advocates of progress in the methods and content of religious education have been criticized and sometimes justly. These criticisms should be squarely faced, for religious education is not a supplanting of anything that is good and true, neither is it a fetish to do the work of grace in men's hearts. By keeping in mind the goals to be sought by religious education the shortcomings complained of will be avoided. There are unlovely qualities in human nature that threaten the success of any church work by criticism of work and worker which can be met if we put the supreme emphasis upon the spiritual results we seek in ourselves and others.

## Questions for Further Study

1. Canvass the leadership of your church and list their opinions upon the religious education movement.

2. Prepare a paper upon the spiritual assets to be looked for from a church program of religious education.

3. Study the situation in some local church school, and list the hindrances and helps to spiritual attainment that you can discover.

4. Block out a program for a Fall Retreat that is designed to give spiritual uplift.

# BIBLIOGRAPHY

# BIBLIOGRAPHY

### Chapter I

"Shall We Stand by the Church?" Durant Drake. Macmillan.

"Democracy and Education," John Dewey. Macmillan, 1922.

"Religious Education and American Democracy," Walter S. Athearn. Pilgrim Press, 1917.

"The Teaching Work of the Church." Association Press, 1923.

"The Religious Education of an American Citizen," Francis C. Peabody. Macmillan, 1917.

"How to Teach Religion," George H. Betts. Abingdon Press, 1919.

### Chapter II

"Religious Education and the Public School," George U. Wenner. American Tract Society, 1913.

"Religious Freedom in American Education," Joseph H. Crooker. American Unitarian Association, 1903.

"A Text-book in the History of Education," Paul Monroe. Macmillan, 1911.

"A History of Religious Education in Recent Times," Arlo A. Brown. Abingdon Press, 1923.

"The Evolution of the Sunday School," Henry F. Cope. Pilgrim Press, 1911.

"Principles and Ideals for the Sunday School," E. D. Burton and Shailer Mathews. University of Chicago Press, 1907.

### Chapter III

"Method in Teaching Religion," George H. Betts and Marion O. Hawthorne. Abingdon Press, 1925.

"Motives and Expression in Religious Education," Charles S. Ikenberry. Doran, 1922.

" Personal and Ideal Elements in Education for Character," Frank C. Sharp.  Bobbs-Merrill, 1917.

" An Integrated Program of Religious Education," W. A. Harper. Macmillan, 1926.

" Principles of Religious Education," E. E. Emme and P. R. Stevick.  Macmillan, 1926.

CHAPTER IV

" Religious Education in the Church," Henry F. Cope, Scribner, 1918.

" The Educational Task of the Local Church," William C. Bower. Front Rank Press, 1921.

" Religious Education and American Democracy," Walter S. Athearn.  Pilgrim Press, 1917.

" Educational Values," William C. Bagley.  Macmillan, 1912.

CHAPTER V

" The Curriculum," Franklin Bobbitt.  Houghton Mifflin, 1918.

" Democracy and Education," John Dewey.  Macmillan, 1917.

" The Curriculum of Religious Education," William C. Bower. Scribner, 1925.

" The Curriculum of Religious Education," George H. Betts. Abingdon Press, 1924.

" One Hundred Projects for the Church School," Milton C. Towner.  Doran, 1925.

" Project Principle in Religious Education," Mason Crum.  Cokesbury Press, 1924.

CHAPTER VI

" Being a Christian," Robert A. Ashworth.  Judson Press, 1924.

" Manual for Training in Worship," Hugh Hartshorne.  Scribner, 1924.

" Story-Worship Programs for the Church School Year," Jay S. Stowell.  Doran, 1920.

" Stories for Worship and How to Follow Them Up," Hugh Hartshorne. Scribner, 1921.

" The Devotional Life of the Sunday School Worker," Charles W. Brewbaker. Revell, 1917.

" Worship in Drama," Charles A. Boyd. Judson Press, 1924.

" Songs for Little People," Frances W. Danielson and Grace W. Conant. Pilgrim Press, 1915.

" Hymn Stories for Children," Margaret Eggleston. Century Co., 1923.

" Religious Education Music Manual," Lucy Carolyn Main. Judson Press, 1927.

### CHAPTER VII

" What Men Live By: Work, Play, Love, Worship," Richard C. Cabot. Houghton Mifflin, 1914.

" What Ails Our Youth? " George A. Coe. Scribner, 1924.

" The Bible Class and the Community," John A. Cross. Revell, 1923.

" Good Times for Girls," Mary E. Moxcey. Methodist Book Concern, 1920.

" Ice-Breakers and the Ice-Breaker Herself," Edna Geister. Doran, 1922.

" The Worst Boys in Town," James L. Hill. Stratford Co., 1919.

" Education Through Play," Henry S. Curtis. Macmillan, 1915.

" The Church and the People's Play," Henry A. Atkinson. Pilgrim Press, 1915.

" How to Conduct Family Worship," Harold M. Robinson. Westminster Press, 1923.

### CHAPTER VIII

" Building a Community," Samuel Zane Batten. Judson Press, 1922.

" Christianity and the Social Crisis," Walter Rauschenbush. Macmillan, 1924.

" Missionary Education in Home and School," Ralph E. Diffendorfer. Abingdon Press, 1917.

" Making a Missionary Church," Stacy R. Warburton. Judson Press, 1924.

" Missionary Education in the Local Church," Herbert W. Hines. Northern Baptist Convention, 1925.

### Chapter IX

" How to Run a Little Sunday School," Edmund M. Fergusson. Revell, 1916.

" Methods of Church School Administration," Howard J. Gee. Revell, 1920.

" Organizing the Church School," Henry F. Cope. Doran, 1923.

" The Graded Sunday School in Principle and Practice," Henry H. Meyer. Eaton and Mains, 1910.

### Chapter X

" Enlisting for Christ and the Church," Howard A. Johnston. Association Press, 1919.

" The Meaning of Faith," Henry E. Fosdick. Judson Press, 1917.

" Letters to Sunday School Teachers," Henry C. King. Pilgrim Press, 1906.

" Evangelism of Youth," Albert H. Gage. Judson Press, 1922.